It's All Relative:
A Perspective Guide to Happiness

Samantha L. DeBruhl

DEDICATION

I dedicate this book to the liberation of all sentient Beings. May we dare to know OurSelf more deeply, share our passions, and expand in love each and every day of our lives.

I also dedicate this book to my soul family and tribe who encouraged me and held space for me to create this guide for all of you. I extend my deepest and sincerest gratitude for those who asked me to speak my truth, long before I know this book existed within me.

For Mom and Dad. You know why...

CONTENTS

ACKNOWLEDGMENTS

This book has unfolded in its own special way that manifested outside of my original plan. There was a point after my mother's death that I put it aside completely unsure if I'd ever publish it. I want to thank Sandy Martin for reaching out one day during that time and asking me when she could read my book. If it wasn't for her, it may still be sitting in a file on a computer for my eyes only.

I also want to thank Lily Sanchez for her passionate dedication to the graphic design and cover art that made this book truly unique. Pictures are indeed worth a thousand words. Thank you Renee Speir for being a second pair of eyes to edit my work. Thank you Tomy Barba for intuitive counsel and helping me to remember my way and planting the seed of an idea for this book years ago. Thank you Keana Parker Photography for capturing my essence in photo form and for empowering women everywhere.

Thank you to my grandparents, Betty Jo and James Carden, who are a beautiful example of unconditional love and support, and who's relationship continues to inspire me. Thank you to my family, my brother James and Uncle Jimmy, who remind me that family doesn't have to be large to be sweet. Thank you for my best friend, Caitlin Dawson, who for the past 8 years has been with me every step of the way. Thank you for seeing me through loving eyes at my lows and believing in my highs. You are my rock.

Thank you to my pet companion and familiar, Wilbur. You are an angel on Earth and I'm so lucky to have you for company on this walk of life. Thank you to my parents in spirit who continue to support me, teach me, and guide me. Thank you Shankar Singh for believing in me, my dreams, and this journey. Thank you for loving me in a way that I felt free. Thank you Brandon Harley for the lessons, reawakening my love, and for loving me deeply. You'll forever have permanent real estate in my heart.

Thank you to all of my friends and loved ones who have played roles in this journey that allowed the lessons to unfold. Thank you for the fairy tale.

A SHIFT IN PERSPECTIVE:
An Introduction

In any given moment, we have millions of different things that we could choose to focus on. What causes our focus to be directed toward certain things and overlook others? How can we shift our attention from thinking and doing to feeling and Being? How can we bring more awareness to the joy in life, and transition from a life of surviving to a life of THRIVING? The shift begins here. It begins within you, and it is reflected as a guide here on these pages.

We exist in a world where the only constant is change. We are constantly evolving and growing as life progresses. Through grace, ease, and sometimes discomfort, we expand into the fullness of our potential. Our resistance to our inner calling often translates into suffering. As a human family, we are in a space of paradigm shift where old conditioning and societal expectations are no longer serving us. Our conditioned thoughts surrounding success are often shaped by what our culture and society have programed in us as their definition of achievement, and not necessarily fulfillment.

Now is an opportunity to unfold a new sense of success that is available to anyone and everyone, yet is unique for you. Many of us have felt burdened by the expectations of previous

1

generations defining success for us, the present generation, as a restrictive linear life path. This path to traditional "success" could include, but is not limited to: going to school to get a job, going to work to pay for school, buying a home that you may not have as much time to enjoy because you are busy going to work to pay the mortgage, investing money into style to impress people you don't even enjoy being in the company of, having a child and passing your legacy onto them and then encouraging them to do the same. This is societal conditioning.

When we shift from putting all of the energy that we historically put into things that were unfulfilling and begin to pour our enthusiasm into following our bliss, our lives are transformed. We discover that our needs become provided for with less "work" and more ease, we liberate ourselves from limiting thought forms, and, by sharing our bliss, we invite others to do the same.

"But my life is different, you don't understand," "I have responsibilities," "Changing my life at this point is too difficult, it is too late," "I have to wait until a, b, or c to do something like this." These are excuses I have heard from my clients over the years, and I can only say that there is no better time to start a shift in perspective than now. By dissolving these limiting binds, you will expand into your potential, and once you do, you'll wish you had started sooner. You will be excited to share your enthusiasm with the world.

We often fear chasing our dreams or following our hearts. Is it because we are not the best at our craft right from the start? We often sell ourselves short and make excuses until we deny that it was our dream all together. Yes, sometimes we outgrow our dreams, or perhaps we experience as much as we desire with one interest and then start on a new dream, but we must be honest with ourselves. Are we choosing a new dream and direction based on inner guidance and new inspiration, or are we giving up because of fear? What causes some of us to give up and some of us to keep pursuing our dreams? Most of all, why would we settle for a status or situation that is stagnant? It's human nature to want to feel safe and secure, but is holding onto something, resisting its evolution, really safe? Making friends with familiarity is a comforting situation, yet how do we ignore that restlessness in our hearts to aspire to what we really want? It is easy to feel comfortable and complacent in a familiar way of living, but it is only by stepping over the threshold of our comfort zone that we find the courage to grant ourselves the dreams that we hold in our hearts. It is with this step that we wake our dreams into reality. It is here that we break down the walls of limitation and find our infinite and expansive potential to create the life we had only imagined.

FORGIVE YOUR HISTORY.
WHERE DO YOU WANT TO GO?

"Because you are alive, everything is possible"
—Thich Nhat Hanh

It is easy to feel limited when we feel like victims of our life-situation. For some of us, the struggle started as early as childhood, and for others it started in early adulthood when we found ourselves graduating high school and just trying to make ends meet while moving forward. We can find challenges in our relationships, in our careers, in disease, illness, and injury; Ultimately, we could find them anywhere.

A powerful shift I experienced during my college years changed my life forever: I discovered life wasn't happening *to* me, it was happening *for* me and through me. I realized we are not victims of our reality, rather that we are co-creating it with our thoughts and perspectives, every moment, every day. In lesson 78 of *A Course in Miracles,* it is mentioned that every moment we have a choice between a grievance and a miracle. Therefore, every perceived burden has potential to be a beautiful blessing, and we are directing our focus and choosing which one we see.

For me, this shift started with taking responsibility for my life. This can seem like a heavy load. The irony, however, is that it is immediately liberating. Recognizing when we choose to perceive events as grievances instead of miracles immediately creates awareness and empowers us to change the lens on the perspective with which we view the world.

Early in my adolescence, I started feeling depressed. Like any concerned parent, my mother decided to take me to see a therapist. In the beginning, my sessions were helpful and I felt like I was getting a grip on my life and healing past wounds. As I transitioned into high school, my therapist decided anti-depressants, mood stabilizers, and anti-anxiety medications would help me to cope with reality and my feelings of sadness. With this advice came a diagnosis of manic depression, bipolar disorder, and panic disorder.

Depression ran in my family. My mother had it, as did my grandmother, and even my great-grandmother. This seemed like a hereditary cross I was destined to bare. I started feeling more depressed, and life often felt heavy and overwhelming. I would experience panic attacks every couple of weeks during which I'd feel like my heart was pounding out of my chest. I would begin counting my heartbeats, certain I was dying, until I passed out or took my anti-anxiety medication. There were quite a few occasions when I was disappointed that the anxiety attack didn't result in my demise. This reflection can seem dramatic to some, but for my former self, this was a reality.

As I got into college, things escalated more. I was away from my house of the past 18 years and was diving into an unknown culture that was supposed to be the key for a successful future. I felt pressured to do my best and feared failure. As I began dating, I was often told I was too emotional, intense, or "crazy", and I began to feel more lost than ever. How was I going to handle my emotions to integrate into this world? I have always been emotional. As an infant, I cried all the time. As a young child, I used my emotions in creative ways by drawing, dancing, singing, and performing plays. As an adult, I had reached a point where I could not control myself, or my emotions, and many people expressed how this inconvenienced them in some way.

I continued to go to psychologists, therapists and psychiatrists for eight years. Every year I would get a new doctor who would prescribe me a cocktail of pharmaceuticals that they had great hopes would help stabilize me. At one point, one of my doctors told me that my cortisol levels skyrocketed because of my stressful perception of reality, and that I would most likely be on the pills for the rest of my life. He also told me I'd most likely never be able to have children because of the birth defects the pills would cause, and it was unlikely that I could handle being off of them. Also, according to him, I most likely wouldn't live past forty if my cholesterol levels didn't get healthier. Of course, to a person already diagnosed as depressed, this news only brought more misery. I gained 100 pounds between my sophomore and junior years of college, and I was miserable.

Feeling sad once in a while or having a bad day does not begin to hint at the grip depression can have on you. Once you feel gripped by a deepening sense of dispassion and intense sadness, your emotions can easily evolve into apathy and leave you disinterested in living at all. There are days that I cursed the sun for shining on my face. I didn't know if I was annoyed more by waking to see another day or that the sun decided to greet me. At times, the depression could be so overwhelming that I would lie in bed and debate if I even wanted to get up to go pee. It was an actual thought process of consideration. *"Do I feel like getting up? That takes too much effort. It's hard enough just to breathe. What if I just peed right here? I could roll over and just go to back to bed on the other side."* This inner discussion was usually followed by a deep sigh, and eventually I would muster up enough effort to go to the bathroom. It is not that in these moments a depressed person does not realize that it is not normal behavior to considering peeing in the bed because it is too exhausting to move; More so, it is that depression can feel so heavy that they ration their energy while battling apathy.

The more my disinterest grew, the more numbing medications were prescribed and integrated into my system. My lover at the time approached me one day and asked, "Do you know we haven't had sex in four months?" Of course I didn't. At that point, I was numb to the world. I kept trying to study my peers and be more like them in hopes that I might appear less "crazy", and eventually I just stopped feeling much of anything. I couldn't even orgasm, so in my chemical cocktail numbness, my sex drive ceased to exist. In an eight-year-period, I was on over ten different medications at different times, and then I began having seizures.

Little did I know at that time that seizures would be my catalyst to a shift in awakening my perception of the world. After missing work a number of times for these medical-related events, my boss suggested I get an FMLA (Family Medical Leave Act) document signed by my psychiatrist to protect me from getting fired for missing work because of this new condition.

The next day, I took the request forms to my psychiatrist and asked her to sign them so I could keep my job. This particular psychiatrist had only been seeing me for ten weeks. Every year I got a new resident psychiatrist and this doctor was new to my condition. To my request she responded, "I don't feel that I understand your condition well enough to feel comfortable signing this." I had never felt so much rage and confusion in one moment in all of my life. I retorted, "You feel comfortable prescribing me narcotics and mood stabilizers that are causing these seizures, but you don't feel comfortable signing a document explaining that?" She replied that she would need me to come back a few more times before she would be comfortable signing the forms..

This was the point in which doctors would say I had a "psychotic break". I was frustrated that I wasn't getting through to the doctors, I felt trapped in the system, and I still wasn't happy. I wanted help and the people that I thought would help me, from my perspective at the time, had failed me. I started arguing, which brought in another doctor who supported my psychiatrist and said that they only reason I was having this emotional episode was because I wasn't being compliant with my medications. Admittedly, once I started having seizures, I started taking less of the mood stabilizer because I felt it was to blame for the reoccurring seizures.

What the doctors saw as a psychotic break was what I describe, in retrospect, as my awakening. Despite this rage, there was an ubiquitous sense of clarity. Feeling betrayed by the people who had degrees and certificates that supposedly meant they could help heal me, I proclaimed that I would not be returning there and that I was getting off *all* of the medication. There was something horribly wrong with this dynamic and situation, and I needed to understand what had happened to me. Who was I anymore? I didn't even know.

That same day, I found a new therapist and shared my desires to stop taking all of the medication that I had been on for the past eight years. I told her my situation and that I wanted to do it responsibly, which meant I needed medical supervision and support. She was hesitant at first, glancing at all of the files from the past eight years that I had given her when I first arrived. Then she said, "I don't agree with your choice, but I support you in making this change responsibly with medical supervision. All I ask is that you meet with me every two weeks, that you be honest with me on how you are feeling, and call me or the Suicide Prevention Line if you have any suicidal thoughts." Deal.

I saw my therapist every two weeks for three-and-a-half months, slowly and steadily reducing my dosage to sobriety. Even better, I hadn't had another seizure. Upon my last session, my new psychiatrist told me, "I honestly didn't think you'd do it. Just promise me if anything changes, you'll call me". I happily agreed.

As the months passed, I started to see the world in an entirely different way. I started really *feeling* my emotions for the first time in eight years. It was intense, surprising, and beautiful. I fought to embrace these emotions and experience life with sobriety, and I felt rewarded for my courage.

After I got off all of the medication, I began witnessing reality in a new way. When I would feel things, I noticed that I began discerning whether the feelings were mine or if I was feeling for my environment. I didn't feel depressed anymore I felt amazed. The more I began acclimating to a life without pills, I felt liberated from the life sentence one of my doctors previously prescribed. I felt EVERYTHING. I felt things intensely for the first times in years, and each feeling was like a gift. As I monitored my emotions, I started recognizing my ability to also feel what others were feeling with great empathy. I experienced so much empathy, in fact, that I was feeling many of the emotions for others. I was like an emotional sponge.

I would feel something, recognize that the emotion was not my own or belonging to my situation, and by creating space within myself, I quickly became able to identify who the emotions belonged to. I soon discovered that people didn't necessarily have to be in my vicinity for me to feel them. I was sensitive. I could wake up on the morning feeling down, take a few deep breaths and then someone would come into my thought-awareness. I started experimenting by reaching out to these people and asking them how they felt, only to find my identification accurate more and more often.

For years I had been medicating a gift that essentially helps me to connect with humanity in ways I didn't realize were possible. Feeling and emotions were my *gift*, not my curse, and these eight years of experience didn't happen to me, they happened *for* me. Later in life, I was able to reflect on this with great reverence, how each person played their role in assisting with my expanded awareness and awakening. I even looked back in gratitude for how difficult my psychiatrist was, because if it wasn't for that event, I could still be in the system, spiraling downward. How many other people are out there thinking they are "crazy" and being medicated just because they didn't understand how to separate their feelings from others? How many other empathic people are out there in the world?

About 5 months after I started my new life of sobriety, I experienced my first sober heartbreak and it was devastating. I called my best friend in intense emotional upheaval and told her that I thought I needed to go back on my medication. This break-up had me anxiety-ridden, and was so different from my other break-up experiences. My best friend pointed out that this was the first challenging life event that I had had since I stopped taking all of the medications, and that I was feeling for the first time what a break-up truly feels like. She told me she supported any decision I would make, but preferred that I just reach out to her so I could work through my emotions within the bounds of my new emotional clarity.

I took her advice, and am so thankful I did. I took a season of solitude and developed a meditation practice. Through meditation, I discovered that my breath tapped me into an omnipresent state of stillness in which I did not feel overwhelmed by my thoughts. I fired the internal judge and instead hired a witness to my thoughts. I also decided to dedicate my energy into something constructive and committed myself fully to my health. Within a two to three year period, I lost the 100 pounds I had gained during my season of depression, and gained an entirely new lifestyle. I was stronger than ever before in mind, body, and spirit. (I discuss in a later chapter, my relationship with food and the tools I gained to create a healthier lifestyle.)

The reason I mention these events is not to give you a biography. It is to aid in a shift of perspective that is available to all of us. If someone would have told me ten years ago that all the time and sadness I spent in therapy would be replaced with happiness and days of peace, I would have never believed them. It's funny how things change, and one day it will all make sense. I know there are some of you out there who think that happiness is impossible or that depression is forever, but I promise, it can get better.

Life is full of so much magic and love, and if you knew how protected and loved you are during your toughest times, you would never be scared again. There were times I remember not wanting to be alive. Not that I wanted to hurt myself to make that so, but that my emotions and pain were so immense I felt they were going to crush me. There were days that panic attacks had my heart beating so hard and so fast and my head spinning so uneasy that I would pray that the "heart attack" I was having would end me because I couldn't stand how long it was taking for me to die. If you have ever had a panic attack, you know what I am talking about. It sounds dramatic, but at one point in time it was my dominant reality, and it was a reality I felt no one really understood no matter how many therapists I talked to.

I share this with you not to invoke sadness, but because there are so many silent sufferers out there that feel this and think that it is forever. It is hard to be convinced of hope while in the depths of sadness, but I promise you, this is not the end, and there is so much more to life than all the sadness and fear you feel. If I didn't live it myself, I would not have believed it. Thankfully, I have, and I know bliss to be real. Life is rewarding in time, and if you knew of all the smiles that will replace your tears, you would wonder why you ever had so much fear.

Most of the people who know me, with the exception of a handful of close family and friends, would never know that this was once my story. I live my life in such a passionate state of bliss and love that a few of my life-coaching clients have passively said, "You don't understand my situation (depression), you are ALWAYS happy!"

How have those people only seen my happiness when I have a history of great disoriented sadness? Once I began taking responsibility for my life and focusing on what I wanted instead of what I didn't want, my life situation up until that point ceased to exist. My past did not define me or my future. The less ego-identified I was with my history or experiences, the less people saw those elements when they looked at me. What I choose to think about in the present is what matters most, and that state of being radiates out of every pore of my body. I felt this historical reflection was a necessary part of this book because there are many people suffering in a relatable way and they wonder if there's a light at the end of the tunnel. I am here, alive and vibrant in vulnerable expression to tell you that there is a light, there is hope, and it DOES get better!

I feel it is important to mention that I am not a medical doctor. I speak from my own firsthand experience, one that is unique to my life path but has the opportunity to resonate with many others in similar circumstances. I am not anti-medication or suggesting that my choice to get off medication is a prescription for anyone who relates with my story, however, I am letting you know there are paths to healing that doctors may not be telling you about. Medication can be a wonderful healing tool, but often times it is abused or used as a coping tool instead of a healing device and people can get stuck there. **Do not ever stop taking medication without a medical professional's supervision.**

It does not make you weak to ask for help and use healthily prescribed treatment in the desire for a cure. It is important, though, to make your decisions as consciously as you can. Our state of consciousness is constantly evolving, and the best we can do is work from the highest consciousness we have access to in each moment. We are all complete with an inner wisdom keeper, a place of self-referral that we often dismiss when listening to everyone else's opinions. I urge you to check in with that often and know that your own personal truth, that most intimate part of your soul, will offer you more healing opportunity than any teacher's gospel.

The more sensitive you are, and the more sensitive you become in life, it is helpful to be mindful of your feelings and be willing to make healthy modifications. Sometimes a sensitive heart has to be sensitive to its own needs and take extra care of Self in order to better integrate into such an intense world. As I become increasingly sensitive to the world around me, I modify my environment, relationships, eating style and situations accordingly. It's important to avoid things that are perceivably harsh, and take time to rest and repair so that you can thrive instead of simply surviving.

Everyone has a different path, but each path has a similar underlying value: infinite potential for growth, expansion, and success, as well as an opportunity to dive deeper into love and act with compassion. This book aims to help you awaken these elements in you. They already exist; They are just waiting to be stirred from their slumber.

THE VOICES IN OUR HEAD

"Out beyond ideas of wrongdoing and right doing there is a field. I'll meet you there. When the soul lies down in the grass the world is too full to talk about it"
-Rumi

When our thoughts are incessant, seldom do we take the time to ask whose voice it is in our head and where it came from. We assume it is our own and that it belongs to us, and therefore trust it without question. It wasn't until I began a meditation practice that I discovered that the voice in my head and the listener were two separate sources. As I began to witness my thoughts, I started recognizing the common mistruths that walked through my mind on the daily. Judgments ruled my mind and I saw how this rigid thought pattern sought to separate me from the rest of the world.

I had judgments about which foods were healthy and unhealthy, I had judgments on what healthy relationships should look like, I had strong opinions that I didn't even feel like voicing because my ego was so sure of itself it didn't even need the validation. Judgments are not to be confused with discernments. Judgments close the mind to new information, while discernments use the information given to make the best decision at that given time. Judgments make someone right and someone else wrong, while discernments suggest a self-loving, more humble approach to decision making.

As my meditation practice grew, I began to watch the thoughts without any attachments and, oftentimes, I would laugh at myself in a childlike innocence, amused that these thoughts were happening. Then I started witnessing my fearful thoughts, and this sparked my curiosity to dive deeper into where they came from.

I could trace much of my incessant background dialogue to my childhood and the voice of my mother. My mother is one of the most compassionate, kind-hearted individuals you could ever meet, however, she does not practice compassion toward herself. As a child, I often listened to her talk to herself aloud, beating herself up for the tiniest things. Her self-talk was damaging and very fearful. As I grew up and watched, I subconsciously adopted her self-talk and her fears; I never really questioned why I didn't like certain foods that I had never tried, or had fears of people that I had no firsthand experience with.

Tracing my thoughts back to my childhood influences, I felt liberated and empowered! These thoughts were not mine, and now I could set them free. Surely it is easier said than done, but awareness was half the battle. This awareness even created a powerful ripple effect backwards in my lineage. My family had a certain way of speaking that did not really empower them or bring them joy. With my own self discovery, I was able to compassionately observe and be an example which began to influence the behavior of my family. Without my unconscious reaction to old patterns, the dynamic was destined to change the structure.

Be cautious of the thoughts you speak aloud, they are the seeds that take root as the inner voice of others. Use your power to make flowers, not weeds.

I began to question everything, not with forceful interrogation, but with inspired curiosity. In questioning myself and my patterns, I was able to recognize which thoughts and habits served me and also identify what I unconsciously adopted during my childhood. As I awakened in self discovery, my family started to question me, both overtly and silently, and ultimately began asking themselves the same questions. Three generations of depression diagnoses were not necessarily biological; They were largely conditional. As my cells began to awaken, the consciousness was igniting clear knowing in those around me. By turning their vision inward, they were also able to recognize patterns and liberate themselves from their prison of damaging self-talk.

This transformation wasn't something anyone would need to jump on a soapbox and preach to the masses about to create change. It was something ignited through the simple act of Presence. Early in my shift of perception, I began reading Eckhart Tolle's *A New Earth*. Tolle has a graceful presence in his writing that is contagious to the reader. It creates stillness in your mind and presence in your being. One of the most powerful quotes I recall from his writings is, "If you want to test your enlightenment, spend a week with your family." When I first read this, I didn't quite understand the challenge he was hinting at. What I came to find, though, was that even though I had found peace within myself, my family had no knowing of this and was patterned in treating me in the way they always had my whole life. It was only through stillness and breaking the patterns of reactivity that I was able to sustain my own peace.

When you are making personal changes, it often takes time for your outer reality to adjust to your new way of living. We teach people how to treat us. When they are used to treating us one way and then we present a new pattern, this can create resistance and, often times, conflict. Often people are resistant to change because it feels uncomfortable and unfamiliar. When we stand strong in change, people who cannot survive in the new dynamic will either leave, seek to pull you back into the old dynamic, or eventually change with you.

I see this as a personal graduation in life. It is bittersweet in a similar way that high school graduation can be. You recognize you are moving forward and evolving, but you know you will not see some of your peers ever again.

As we grow and experience, sometimes our perception of reality can invite an overwhelming amount of stress into our lives. Without healthy tools, we can spiral into anxiety, create dis-ease in our bodies, and even adopt vices or develop an addiction. Anxiety arises from concerns relating to the future, and worry comes from perceptions of our past experiences. Neither are in the present moment, and therefore, worry and anxiety do not serve to help us in the Now. The present moment is the only reality and the only place we can commune with our souls. The mindful practice of meditation helps to create space where we cannot seem to find any in our active lives, and places our attention in the present. By tuning into our life-force breath, we tap into a vital tool that is always accessible to calm our nervous system, our mind, and ultimately, our whole body.

To begin meditating, find a comfortable place to sit or lie down. You can do this almost anywhere, but to start a practice, it is ideal to start in someplace familiar, comfortable, and where you feel that you won't be disturbed. Close your eyes and connect to your breath. Try not to judge your breath or the thoughts that arise in your mind; Just allow yourself to inhale deeply and exhale. It is important not to get too caught up in thoughts about breathing or whether you are doing it "right". It is only important that you are passively engaged with your breath. In time, this will become more natural and you will be able to drop into a meditative state with ease.

There is really no wrong way to meditate. There are more effective ways, and this will be validated by the level of peace you experience during your practice. While staying connected to your breath, you can witness the flow of inhale and exhale, deepening your breath, and then allow your breath to flow passively in and out. You can even try connecting your flow of inhale to exhale by making a smooth transition of breath that allows them to weave together, dissolving the need to identify which came first.

The more present you are with your breath, the less need there will be to attach to the thoughts drifting through your mind. Your thoughts may rise and subside, and sometimes you may even drift away from your breath for a brief time as you entertain a thought. Smile and return to your breath. Your thoughts will become less and less. The first time I asked myself, "Who is thinking these thoughts?" a lovely shift in consciousness happened. You may try that, as well, if you feel inspired and see what you experience for yourself.

I often meditate for an hour or two when I am devoted to my practice, but at minimum, I meditate for at least 20 minutes a day. When I worked in a hospital trauma center, I would often find myself making excuses as to why I did not have time to meditate. Trying to balance my schedule, meditation would drop down to the bottom of my list of priorities, and I found my stress levels increasing. When I began to honor my meditation practice as a top priority, I felt more balanced, and I was more productive throughout my day.

There is an old Zen adage that says, "You should sit in meditation for 20 minutes a day, unless you're too busy; then you should sit for an hour." The truth is, when you meditate, time dissolves, and with a centered state of grace, you find more clarity and organization which allows your days to be more productive with less "work".

Meditation is a pathway to the innermost workings of your soul and your true self. In meditation, you can shift your perception, dissolve untruths, and decode confusion. You become more of what is "real" and less of what is illusion. You are able to identify your ego and its design to work as a servant to Spirit, unlike the reversed role it tends to play in our unconscious state of living. By checking in with our witness, we develop a growing clarity of what we want and what we need in our lives. There is less fear surrounding speaking our truth and desires, and in times of fear we can shift the perception from an obstacle to a stepping stone on our path to our heart's desires. Our life journey is not a battle of ego and consciousness. It is about recognizing the true self from the servant of self. The mind is a servant to Spirit, and oftentimes we can become wayward and disillusioned in mistaking the mind as the only Self. There are an infinite number or potential outcomes and experiences you can have during meditation. As you experience expansion into the infinite, you are also able to understand an infinite depth within you. Your perception of the Universe transcends the seen Universe and expands infinitely within and without.

Although meditation is a state of opening and listening as opposed to the speaking and requesting as we commonly do in prayer, I like to open my meditations with an intention. I have many intentions I have used over the years, but one of my favorite opening prayers is the Asatoma prayer.:

Lead me from the unreal to the real,
from the darkness to the light,
from the time bound state of consciousness
to the timeless state of Being.

From here, I will fall into my breath, become witness to my mind, and listen to my expanding consciousness to experience a greater state of peace.

TO UNITE OR TO BE RIGHT

"We can heal our broken world when we give up the need to be right"
—India Arie

If you arrive at an obstacle with a defensive strategy, you are unable to remain open to the healing that Presence and stillness can bring. Many times we will be so fixed in a belief that we judge ourselves as right, and others who do not see it our way as "wrong". This prevents the opportunity for compassion to mend the separation of seemingly opposing forces. By responding with tension and conflict in mind and body, even if your argument is morally sound, you are contributing to the dis-ease of the whole.

For example, I have many friends who are animal activists as well as passionate vegans. I wholeheartedly support saving animal lives and being compassionate to sentient beings, but at times this passion can present itself as evangelical. When we are teaching and sharing our knowledge and perspective, it is important to arrive in equality rather than raising a platform for patronizing view points. If you want to invite someone to share in something that you find beneficial, be it a belief, event, lifestyle, and so on, you want to build a bridge with harmony, otherwise, you are further separating yourself from peace and union with humanity.

People at peace with themselves do not look for conflict outside of themselves. A person who has experienced awakening to God-consciousness understands there are an unlimited amount of pathways for someone to share the same experience. Discounting someone who has differing belief systems from you further separates you from the grace of Spirit and grossly underestimates the ability of Spirit to speak through any given modality.

One does not necessarily have to believe exactly what another does to experience great peace. One merely has to extend compassion where understanding and relation seems to have escaped them. In this act, you discontinue the unconscious act of being a mirror to someone else's behavior, and instead become a window into the space where Spirit resides.

The human condition is that we often learn and grow through opposites. To learn compassion and love, we experience what it feels like to feel unloved. To develop trust, we often experience betrayal. To experience relationships with others in a healthier way, we learn in contrast with experiences of solidarity, sometimes loneliness, or a sequence of unhealthy relationships. By experiencing these challenges, we are able to relate to the suffering of others, dissolving separateness, and are then able to compassionately see ourselves in another.

The more we experience, the more pathways we have to relate to one another on the planet, and ultimately, the more empathy we have to lend toward acts of compassion. Through our own suffering, we have firsthand experience with pain, and even if we don't live in that suffering anymore, we still have memories of the pain and are reminded when we see suffering reflected back to us in the face of humanity.
Experiences are not designed to make us suffer. Experience is a neutral term. It is through our perception that we identify an experience as good or bad, painful or comforting. All

experience is a pathway to unity. Unity is where we came from, and unity is where we will return. We invite this voluntary state of amnesia to know ourselves more deeply. This is where experience comes in to educate us, thrill us, break down what is not real, only to reveal the truth that remains.

There is only one of "us" here. With voluntary amnesia, we start to view ourselves as separate to engage in a human experience. The human experience includes a very unique kind of suffering that we do not experience without incarnating on Earth. We consciously choose this experience and contract with other "parts" of our Self to heal us or awaken us back to a reality of oneness and unity.

When "someone else" is in a rage, this is their clearing of human conditioning and an opportunity for healing and awakening. With purging of projections and unhealthy emotions, there is space made for light, knowing, and peace. It is our conscious duty to not fill it back up with rage but allow light to fill that space with our presence. It is as if we are one organism, like the human body, for example. A person in our awareness that is suffering in anger is like our arm that fell asleep from being laid on too long. The reason it is tingling and filling with electric nervous sensation is not as important as it is that the body immediately responds in healing and returning it to a balanced stasis. The body supports healing the sensation not by giving up, but by supporting it in waking back up.

Our ego loves to create stories about everything. If our bodies acted with an ego-response and identified in self serving separations like the ego-mind, there would be chaos and discourse throughout the body's systems. Imagine if the liver were to claim the stomach is lazy and decide it need   or a vacation, or it is going to quit, but the stomac mouth for bringing more work and less help, and blame is cast. Luckily, our ideal healthy bodies w of oneness and with all parts working to keep the whole alive and well. When a part starts to suffer, we call this disease, and just like a disease happens in the body, dis-ease can also be created in the collective body of humanity in the form of poverty, illness, war, violent death, and chaos.

We, at the level of spirit, cannot die. Our physical body can age, die, and decay, but our soul is infinite, timeless, and ongoing. The more we become intimate with this part of us, the more we tap into the infinite potential that we came from and can bring it here to this world.

As a young girl, I was raised in a Christian family. I had endless questions; The more I read the Bible, the more questions I had. One question I dwelled on most was the concept of heaven and hell. I could not understand how the idea of perfection could be the same for everyone, and if it were, how could a utopia exist in the afterlife that is unique to my ideas of perfection *and* coexist with the ideas of perfection of everyone who made it to this place? I also couldn't see how an all loving God could sentence people to eternities in a torturous hell. The more I tapped into my soul-self and lived it daily here on the Earth, I began to feel like I was in the blissful grace that I could only relate to as heaven. That is when I realized that heaven is not necessarily a physical place you go to when you transition from this world; It is something we bring here and, by choice, can experience daily. We can bring heaven, or we can bring hell. It is not a sentence we are given, it is a choice we make, moment by moment, each day of our lives. Heaven is the reality we live when we are feeling closeness with Spirit. We experience hell in separation from Spirit. God consciousness is always available to us, we make a choice with our perception.

Things started to make more sense to me as I lived with Christ consciousness instead of just reading about it. I may have been young, but even as a child, I realized that even though things often got lost in translation, there were still tokens of wisdom to uncover from these teachings.

Time only explained in a linear format for birth, life, and the finality of death is frightening. It was foreign to me because I could always see cycles: I saw seasons, I saw the sun rise and set, I saw the moon wax and wane. What really dies? I wanted to know to understand this linear theory presented to me. People brave enough to live a question are often rewarded by eventually living the answer. Knowing this, I discovered the metaphors woven between all faiths connecting the infinite pathways to spirit in a variety of texts. This wasn't competition, this was interpretation, and this interpretation is what we do everyday of our life to choose heavenly moments or experiences of living hell.

Bringing this wisdom and foresight to the present moment, I felt empowered knowing I had a choice. I could take a playful approach, or a serious one. I could feel like a victim or a co-creator. I could feel lack for what I didn't have or I could feel gratitude for what I did have.

The God-, Source-, Universe-consciousness that before seemed so detached and connected to finality is actually living and breathing here within us each day of our lives, and is accessed through a shift of perception that is available to us in any given moment we choose. Unity is not about right or wrong. It is about dissolving the perspectives that distance us from each other and, ultimately, from God.

So the next time you are confronted with a choice or a potential conflict, you can take a moment to silently ask yourself, "Is it time for me to be right, or is it better to unite?" Then you can build a bridge to unity, or wait on your shore staring at an ocean of possibilities.

This does not mean you should allow someone to treat you poorly, or be walked on like a doormat when an opposing view point surfaces. This just means that you can pick your battles. Is peace more important than being right? Is this serving my ego or is this serving my Spirit? These questions are all gatekeepers to check yourself at the door.

When people want to stop seeing the ugliest perspective available, they learn to change themselves, not the world around them. Changing yourself, though, has the brilliant side effect of changing the world around you.

People often fall into victim mentality where they blame the world around them for their misery. People who choose to be victim of their life situation say things such as, "This happened *to* me," and "Woe is me." They choose to be offended by everything or look for the nasty side of any given perspective. This is not necessarily a true view of reality. If you choose to see the blessing in the burden, this does not mean you are in denial. Your perception of the world is seen through the clarity of your heart. Some people can find the ugly side of a rainbow and complain that there is not enough black.

Watch where your attention goes. Where do you look? What do you see? Re-pattern yourself to see the beauty and the good. This paints your reality.

When I go out, sometimes I'll hear people criticizing the way someone is dressed or how awful their makeup, hair, or shoes are. I never saw any of this. Why? I am too busy looking at that person's beautiful smile, the way a young lady opens the door for the older gentlemen, or the way the young man smiles with his eyes when he looks at his girlfriend. We can filter what seems invasive to our awareness by watching in mindfulness.

What is being shown and what do we see?

Opportunities to evaluate our perspective of the world are always happening, but when distracted by judgment, people are robbing themselves of the potential to see all of the miracles life has to offer.

The next time you find yourself being critical, find three beautiful things in the same room. Re-pattern. Remember love. Then find something beautiful about yourself, because really this is where judgment starts: negative self-talk.

BEEP BEEP BEEP

"You will not be punished for your anger, you will be punished by your anger."
—Buddha

Reacting with anger is similar to trying to put out a fire with a fire alarm. We all know that water or a fire extinguisher would be more productive, but that does not necessarily get the most attention. Spirit has no interest in who is getting more attention, but the ego loves a raging battle of wits.

Anger can often be deemed a negative emotion. To me, anger presents awareness and signals the body that something is not in alignment. This is often reflected in our external reality and can easily be blamed on the mask outside of us being masqueraded on another. Your personal fire alarm lets you know that there is smoke in your house and flames to follow. Anger in action is when the emotion that was once a signal becomes a responsibility. As a feeling, anger is personal and is a helpful guide in steering us to our places of resistance, and it begs us to identify what is true within us.

Anger often arises when we feel threatened in some way. It can be an emotional threat: betrayal, heartbreak, competition. It can be a physical threat: pain, entrapment, limitations, failing health, or lack of necessities. Anger arises in defense of an opposition, and can create a greater conflict if not monitored. Making friends with your anger is like recognizing the fire alarm before the fire burns down your house. It is a tool and an aid if you invite it to be.

When anger rises up within me, I shower it with gratitude. I am so thankful to know that something has sparked a fire, and I dig deeply into my emotional wound or perceived physical limitation and ask what I can learn there. It is ok to listen to the fire alarm, but to act on it won't heal the trespasses. The alarm will just get louder and louder until your house, or the situation, burns down, or until you can find a solution and extinguish the flames with a better tool.

Anger gets our attention with discomfort. It ceases to be uncomfortable when we respond with a reaction from our heart center. Anger intensifies the more our ego feels threatened by the opposition or trigger. Where have we become separated in the dynamic?

It is difficult to not be reactive, but the more we are able to zoom out on a big pictures perspective, the less this trigger seems to shake our whole world. Intense emotions like anger and frustration lack a grander wide lens perspective. It zooms in on the one thing causing conflict and makes it seem like it is all that exists in that moment. If we are able to be fully present when these emotions arise, our breath can expand the limiting frame on this event. Once again using the burning house metaphor, when we zoom out to a big picture perspective, we feel less threatened, and the fire appears more manageable. What once looked like a house burning down was just a small part of one room that can be easily extinguished.

It is important to recognize that being triggered by anger does not make you more or less of a person or Being. It is natural to recognize threatening situations, and conditioning can influence anger as an appropriate response to threats. This inner fire can be tamed, making us less flammable in the future by creating preventative measures in moments where we are not angry.

Creating a sanctuary within helps us to make space for our thoughts and feelings when we are triggered by an outside influence. It is easier to practice this when there is not a person right in front of you at the time of conflict, but you can eventually adopt this new flame extinguishing practice to use in all dynamics. *Before going further, I would like to mention that these exercises are not for practicing when you are in physical danger and you need to protect yourself physically. If you are being attacked or being physically abused by a person or situation, please get help to find protection and safety.*

These tools are used to loosen the grip anger has on us and to make us less reactive, which in turn creates less conflict in our lives. If we don't add fuel to the fire, it will die out more quickly. Next time you are in traffic and you feel triggered by an event - perhaps someone cuts you off when you're running late, maybe someone forgot to use their blinker, maybe someone is honking at you and you don't even know why - find yourself in tune with your breath. When you are focusing on breathing it is difficult to become overwhelmed by emotions. If you can do it, your mind creates more stillness and you are able to zoom out from the moment. You can witness the tantrum or someone else's anger without being caught in the storm. I also like to send a person away with a silent blessing, praying that they safely and peacefully make it to their destination. A great mantra I use when I feel pressure in traffic is, "I am protected, I am safe, and I will arrive in Divine timing." Decreasing the added influence of self-inflicted pressure alleviates the potential for explosive reactions.

A more challenging and transformative practice is when you find yourself in an argument or conflict with a pers front of you. Perhaps it is with a co-worker, boss, friend, parent, or spouse. Our outer world reflects our inner world, so when I experience conflict outside of myself, I zoom out for a bigger picture and feel within. My goal with interactions such as these is to become a window to a peaceful center, when historically I responded as a mirror to the opposition.

When we are able to remain in tune with our breath while listening to someone else's anger, we are making space for transmutation to heal the situation rather than putting up walls and resistance to encourage in further conflict. When we create stillness and remain porous, the feelings can pass through and we can witness without being caught in an unconscious battle. This is not to be mistaken with apathy. Being present is existing in fullness and has a side effect of compassion. Instead of being disconnected, you are fully engaged, but not succumbing to being fully enraged.

I once had a conflict due to miscommunication with a coworker. In her perspective, I had unknowingly been offending her for quite some time, and finally the pressure was too much to stand so she reacted in a rage where she was screaming in expression of her wounded feelings. I was caught off guard but immediately remembered my breath and just listened to everything she had to say. I kept my eye contact fully engaged, and as I listened I was able to recognize where some of her anger was influenced by other events in her life and how I had triggered her unconsciously. Instead of contributing further through reactivity, I became a window instead of a mirror. She may have still seen a mirror in her emotional perspective which fueled her anger, but when the emotions subsided, stillness remained. Without reacting with a like intensity, she was able to relieve the pressure and together we could heal the miscommunication with healthy exchange. We are able to make decisions from a still place within us instead of a reactive temporary emotion.

This is not easy. I am not suggesting that this is something you can do the first time with no challenge, but it is an exercise to strengthen your emotional reactivity and establish new patterns for healing conflict where old patterns have ceased to work. With this self awareness, we become less conflicted within, and therefore attract less conflict in our external world.

During heightened emotional times influenced by hormones, women in particular can feel easily agitated with an increased level of sensitivity. The outer world does not change, but our body chemistry influences how we experience the world around us. This sensitivity can increase around menstrual cycles, also referred to as moon-cycles, and is usually ushered in by a period of time referred to as PMS, or pre-menstrual syndrome.

I have a friend who is very in tune with her emotions and has contributed a great perspective on this type of situation. She is able to recognize when she is being triggered by her hormones and when she is feeling vulnerable or conflicted. She has reclaimed the term PMS and redefined it as "Please Make Space". By recognizing her needs, she can identify how to prevent conflict during highly sensitive times when she may be easily triggered.

Transparent communication is vital in preventing conflict before it happens, and extinguishing it after it occurs. The more we are in tune with our needs and what helps us feel safe, to feel heard, and to feel fulfilled, we are able to communicate with others about how to help us provide that environment. We don't put pressure on others to read our minds, and we don't have to fix things after offenses occur.

Anger can be triggered by feeling vulnerable, but it can also be extinguished by that same vulnerability when used as a catalyst to heal. It is within the consciousness behind that vulnerability that we can find how to feel empowered and liberated by our tenderness, even if historically we felt trapped and threatened, holding on to our needs in silence.

Putting PMS - "Please Make Space" - into action is an exercise, we can do not only with others, but also with ourselves. The more stillness we create within by tuning into our bodies and breath, we create space. The more space we have, the less resistance we experience and the less we are triggered by our external world. By expressing our needs to create more space externally, we invite a comforting solution where this unspoken need once felt threatened.

The intimate experience we have with our inner world directly effects the world around us. By creating a peaceful inner world, we contribute to a peaceful outer world around us. The world is a perfect mirror to us. This mirror is not meant to torture us as we may have once perceived; It is meant to create more awareness of ourselves and to guide us to healthier life experience.

Often conflicts arise when we take things personally. We could trigger someone else, and they could begin an irate torrent of words simply because their inner turmoil is being reflected outside of them and onto your face. This also happens the other way around when we think that someone else is causing our pain but it is merely a mirror that we are looking into that has uncovered a wound from under the surface. This is known as projection, Differentiating between something that is not personal and when something is actually your responsibility will greatly decrease your number of conflicts.

Taking nothing personally is a practice easier said then done, especially if the other actor in the picture projects with great intensity that, "because of YOU I feel this way!" "YOU did 'x', 'y' and 'z' and it is all YOUR fault!" But imagine this: every person is a mirror and the behavior of another is not your reflection. Your reaction is your reflection and it is a choice you make.

The beauty in the chaos is that we signed up for this. We wanted to engage with others as part of a human experience. It is how we learn to know our Self (our Self being our Higher Self and God-consciousness). Once we know our Self all the illusions of conflict, projection, guilt, fear, and victimization are shown for what they are: False participants in a journey to knowing our Self. None of the aforementioned aspects are real, just thoughts about who and what we think we are that we must face and shed to really know our soul and our purpose.

When altercations happen between two souls, we have many options on how to behave and respond, but I always believe that events unfold based on people trying to do the best they can to communicate from their current level of consciousness. This is not saying that anyone is better than the other at any level of consciousness, but that some people are in a more balanced state of alignment to a higher level of presence and consciousness.

The role we take is to hold that mirror up by standing intensely in the present. Others may not always like what they see, but that is because what they see is not real. The stories they have created about themselves and who they are or what they do, is not who or what they *really* are. This false self is slipping from their control and is causing suffering. What they see is a mask of pain, rage, unworthiness. What they see on the mirror that you are to them is a false self, or the ego. But how profound it is to stand there, in love, to be another's reflection? We all do this for each other each and every day. We are love, and when aligned with our true nature we see it reflected everywhere. When we are suffering, our ego craves more pain, and therefore, we find it everywhere.

Sometimes these emotional clearings (high emotions such as crying, screaming, roaring) are the breaking point that lets the light shine in on some real truth. Another person's reactions are never about us. Unless under our own free will we adopt the thoughts of another as our own, they are not about us. Once again, *if anyone ever causes you physical harm, leave immediately as safely as you can.* Eckhart Tolle speaks of this type of "pain body" coming from a very unconscious state. You do not need to be a mirror or a martyr to this type of aggressor; You need to protect yourself. A different kind of healing is necessary in these cases and your role here is self-preservation and your own protection and well being.

As much as emotional and verbal conflicts seem to affect our relationships, know you always have a choice. You can be present in love and be the mirror to help another in their healing, you can choose to take it personally, jump on the ego train and play roles such as the victim from a space of blame, fear, jealousy and all sorts of other "fun" stuff, or you can create healthy loving boundaries and walk away.

Some tips I offer in these situations:

1. Imagine the other as a child. This should not be at all condescending. This is intended to be open-hearted, understanding, and compassionate. As we have all gone through different ages, stages, and levels of consciousness, we can non-judgmentally see the other in this stage of growth that we have already experienced. We have grown through it, and they can

too.

2. Listen. Listen with your ears. Listen with your heart. But most of all, listen without an agenda. This is the doorway to Presence.

3. Know yourSelf. When you know yourSelf the opinions of others will have little or no upset to your inner peace. Your inner peace stands on the foundation of your personal truths.

4. Say to yourself, and know it to be true, "The other is mySelf. I love the other as I love mySelf." This does not come from the ego where things get taken personally, this is recognizing the Divinity in yourself and that reflection in all things.

A person can only participate so long in their personal riot without anyone responding in their desired way. Have you ever sat in stillness while someone is releasing all sorts of emotions and venting chaos in their own personal storm? The storm loves to suck in more fuel for its fury. There is a power in this stillness. Not control, but power. Without the storm being fed, it will acclimate to the most dominant presence in the room: stillness. When a storm dies down, all the shrapnel and debris can be seen with clarity for what it is in the contrast of this powerful stillness. This is when an epiphany happens, and often a shift in consciousness, for the subject in healing. Maybe not immediately, but inevitably. Presence and Love are omnipresent. They are always within us just waiting for us to tap back into them. Therefore, we can only lose what is not real or what is not who we truly are.

Be the Light, not the fuel to the fires of conflict. Believe it or not, being a victim requires your consent and adoption of that role, otherwise, you'd label yourself as "participant". You can choose to be a Divine playmate, a partner in healing, a reflecting pool of love, and a rock star. Like I have said, you have options. (This is not referring to the definition of victim as related to circumstances of a physical or abusive oppression).

Be grateful to yourself and others, everyday, for sharing in healing, emotional and otherwise. Without each other, life would be rather pointless. You may think it would be a lot easier to be enlightened if there were no people. It would also be impossible.

Anger is a signal from your conscious self that something needs attention. It is not a way to act or behave except for those not conscious enough to separate themselves from triggers. We can have awareness of areas that need improvement in the world surrounding us, but being angry about it is simply reenacting the essence of the cause for the current separation from peace in the world.

Recognizing a situation that triggers anger and realizing that it is a place in need of compassion is the key to transforming humanity's lens of reality. We have been conditioned primitively to get angry at what is wrong or unjust, but that is a low vibration reaction and is not healing anything in humanity.

It is likely that most of you have heard the quote from the great Buddha, "Being angry is like holding onto a hot coal and expecting the other [person, thing, event] to get burned."

Anger speaks nothing of the subject and only of the person feeling it. It is up to the experiencer to identify with the anger or see it for the trigger/alarm it is. When I feel anger rise, which is seldom, I ask myself three questions: Who is this serving? Where is this feeling actually coming from? Who is feeling this?

It is amazing to experience the stillness that replaces the turbulent feeling of anger. From that place of stillness you can formulate plans and co-create with the Divine to find solutions for "problems" as we see them in society. "Problem" is another word for a low vibrational perspective of reality as it is. Conscious witnessing sees "opportunity" where ego sees "problems". Conscious viewers see opportunities for healing, awakening, compassionate practice, growth, creation, and thinking-outside-of-the-box. This is the shift in consciousness that leads us to personal peace that eventually transforms into global peace.

When has anger created a solution where anger was also the source of the "problem"? When the mind works from a state of anger, it is in resistance to reality as it is. It is comparable to driving with the breaks on and expecting to get somewhere quickly. Frustration is amplified. Albert Einstein said, "We cannot solve problems with the same thinking that created them". What I take from that quote is that fighting fire with fire only creates more fire [resistance]. Acting from a place of non-resistance or peace in a world of chaos has more transformative power than the former. An angry peacemaker is equivalent to shaking the world you want to be at peace and screaming "Calm down!! Be still!! Why can't you be peaceful like me?!?? *ROAR!!*". The truth is, the world is as peaceful as you are. Events come into your awareness and provide a mirror of opportunity to check your peace. As Deepak Chopra said during his global peace meditation, "The exterior world is a reflection of our inner world. If you don't like the refle/
does not help to break the mirror."

Feeling angry is not right or wrong, it simply is what it is from your current state of consciousness. Know peace within and you will see peace outside.

Once upon a time, my ego presented me with an opportunity. As it gripped my mind by way of a hostile email I received one night, I began experiencing a stream of unpleasant emotions. The first to arrive was frustration, my mind picking away like a pick axe in a mine. Gems? Rocks? I closed my eyes and began to witness each uncomfortable feeling: frustration, pride, insecurity, discontent, anger. I honored each with reverence as a teacher, a traveler, a stranger, a friend. As one arose, the former would subside, like fishermen casting hooks into the sea. In my stillness, I chose to watch, not bite. Falling into my breath, thoughts began to surface: fight for your ego and rights, or surrender to serenity? This is a choice we make.

Looking up into the night sky, I engaged a star in a staring contest. In deep gaze, I began to feel small, so small, the smallest I have ever felt. At that precise moment, with a twinkle and a blink, as I felt I could not be anymore insignificant in size, instantly I expanded. It was if the Big Bang had taken place in my heart. It was if my heart reached the edges of the Universe yet never arrived; Infinite. What once felt small (me), and what felt so large (the situation) swapped places as my Being expanded to all that is, and the "problem" dissolved into an abyss. What was the problem? I could not seem to remember.

We are not situations. We are the awareness of them. Our experience a ripple, not the sea.

FINDING SACRED SPACE

"Your sacred space is where you can find yourself again and again." —
Joseph Campbell

I have spent days meditatively listening to the sky and looking to it as a teacher. I learned lessons from witnessing the clouds. The clouds are always effortlessly changing, impermanent. Sometimes they are dark with rain, sometimes they are fluffy and white. Like most things in nature, they don't resist what is. Therefore nature does not mentally suffer like we do when change arises. The sky does not identify itself by the state of the clouds. The sky simply *is*. It is always in the background, behind the clouds in space and stillness, much like our witnessing mind.

Our inner sacred space is much like the infinite, still, expansive sky. This is the home of our Being and where we connect to our soul and our Divinity. When we make this unseen world our state of Being, this is awakening. This awakening is also referred to as enlightenment. When we are able to live in this space, we are at peace in our soul and our inner world and outer world dissolve into one.

There are many paths to recognizing this space, but this space is always with us. It is us in its infinite, formless form. Many of us have experienced glimpses of this or perhaps have experienced it for a season in time, but then found ourselves feeling disharmony or unease again as we navigate through life. This is not uncommon. To have a sustainable enlightenment experience is somewhat rare yet it is growing in documented cases. I personally believe I cannot consider myself entirely awakened until all that is in awareness is also enlightened. Being interconnected to all things makes everything a part of us and vice versa. Although our primary awareness may be in one form known as our body, the idea of separateness is incompatible with the unity of enlightenment. Parts of the whole can recognize their wholeness in personal enlightenment, but only when the parts dissolve into one awareness will we experience the truth of One.

Until then, we can do our best to achieve personal enlightenment, which by default ripples to all in time. We do this by discovering our sacred space. Sacred space can also be created outside of ourselves in the form of a ritual, temple, church, altar, ceremony, or other various ways to worship. By creating a manifestation of a sacred representation, we are reflecting our desires to create or maintain this sacred space within.

I have been pleasantly surprised by the innumerable ways I have discovered sacred space in my life. Anytime we commune with nature, we can find Spirit. I have found my sacred space in traditional methods through meditation, church, temple, kirtan, sacred sexuality practices, and ritual. I have also found my sacred space in the gym on the treadmill, on a kayak, typing this book, walking my dog, and eating a meal. You can recognize the revealing of this sacred space by the feeling of grace and peace that you experience in the moment. You may also find clarity, Divinely inspired creativity, a solution to an unresolved question, or a feeling of interconnectedness with all things.

I have been going to church since I was an infant. Over time church has taken on many different faces. Recently the gym has been my church. I have been using the treadmill to bring me closer to my Higher Self. As I run, I am open and receptive to intuitive guidance. I am able to use any restless energy in a constructive way and heal my body at the same time.

Church, to me, is any place I surrender to sacredness, where I can commune with god, goddess, all there is with great attention, focus, and intention. Essentially, this is anywhere and everywhere, but I have chosen to enchant my gym to make it more enticing for my transformation and growth. As I strengthen my body, I strengthen my relationship with Spirit by remaining open and receptive to intuitive guidance. I clear a variety of negative thought patterns and am intensely present in the awareness of actions I need to take to move my life in a productive and fulfilling direction. When silencing our busy mind, we are open to messages from our Higher Self that help guide us in life.

One time I was having a difficult time balancing my schedule. My calendar had events in every square and I was feeling drained. One morning on the treadmill, I tapped into my sacred space and received a clear solution from spirit: *refrain from having conversations and hanging out with people out of obligation. Having conversations out of obligation is not a service to you or others. By removing action through obligation you discover your dance through inspiration.*

Of course, there is necessity for function, like paying rent and mortgage, but in many necessities you can find inspiration by shifting your perspective to the aspects of fulfillment. In this conversation with Spirit, I discovered that the business I felt in my life opposed the vibrant sense of inspiration I had once felt doing similar tasks. By not listening to my inner voice, I turned Divinely inspired compassion into a draining obligation. With this clarity and message of truth from my sacred space, I was

45

able to modify my life to be more productive and full of inspiration.

This subject of obligation also relates to a common situation in which people feel obligated to participate in a religious practice or go to a specific place of worship to feel sacred. What once was an inviting opportunity to share space with others in worship can turn into an unfulfilling obligation. People can become obsessed with *doing* instead of *being*. This is where I find people losing interest in things they once loved. They neglect to listen to the calls of their inner voice and forget to follow their heart. The places you can commune with Spirit are infinite and expansive. Don't let limiting thoughts keep you in a place that distances you from peace.

Taoist philosopher Wei Wu Wei once described the unfulfilled devotees of various faiths as "Worshipping the teapot instead of drinking the tea." There is nothing more correct or less correct about following a particular faith if you find peace, joy, love, and fulfillment within it. What Wei Wu Wei speaks of with this quote is that many people busy themselves with the ritual of religion and neglect the sacredness of experiencing Divinity within themselves. I see religion as the belief in another person's spiritual experience, while spirituality is the experience of your own. This also is revealed in the relativity of perspective. We do not have to necessarily go to a sacred space, we *are* the sacred space.

Ideally, when we discover our sacred space within, we recognize the sacred nature of the world around us and find the opportunity to walk in living prayer. However, before this becomes your permanent experiential state, it is essential to take a more practical approach by creating a sacred living space that reflects what sacred means to you. By definition, the word sacred relates to religion, but more importantly, sacredness is where you commune with God, Higher Self, and your Divinity.

The art of Feng Shui is a popular way to create a space with a more favorable energetic affect. You can easily notice how it dramatically changes the feeling in a room when you rearrange furniture. You can practice tapping into your intuition and honor your sensitivities by rearranging your home in a way that feels good as opposed to simply one that simply looks good. Try to let go of logic and move some decorations and furniture around. How does it feel? Often times when things are aligned in a healthy flow, we can feel lighter and experience more ease while breathing. Colors play an important role in creating a mood for a space. Some colors feel intense, while others are soothing. Make sure you put colorful things that you find relaxing in your living space that are conducive to more ease and comfort in your sacred environment. Lighting also affects the feeling and energy of the room. Pay attention to which times of day your space is the most lit and which times are the most dark. Witness how you feel during these times. You can also contribute other lighting tools like candles and lamps to create a mood that is perfect for you.

Our homes are an important sacred space. Although many of us spend more of our waking time away at work than we do at our homes, it is still incredibly important to create a sanctuary that reminds us of Divine nature of peace. I have even taken special consideration to also make my vehicle a sacred space by decorating it with things that influence bliss and ease. I really like the energy of angels, and decorate my car with images and objects that remind me of the presence of angels in my life. I also find the color of light aqua (similar to Robin's egg blue) to be particularly comforting, so I chose a car specifically that color.

We shape our reality, consciously and unconsciously. By creating deliberately and mindfully, we create a paradise here on earth that enables us to live a life of sustainable ease at heart that is also spiritually stimulating.

VULNERABILTY IS A SUPER POWER

"And the day came when the risk to remain tight in a bud was more painful than the risk it took to blossom."
- Anaïs Nin

I talk a lot about being your authentic self, embracing it because that is who you came here to be. Solidarity and reflection has humbled me, as Spirit often does in moments of resistance, and I had to be honest with myself. As much as I am very genuine and sincere in my way of living, there is a lot I filter from the world out of fear of judgment. I feel I know my authentic self very well but I don't express it as much as I am compelled to because that feels vulnerable.

Vulnerability can be a scary place, but also the key to enlightenment, love, and feeling. Ironically, it is the most profound form of strength. Yet, for many of us, allowing ourselves to be vulnerable is an internal battle, like a perfect storm dwelling inside of each of us.

One day, I happened to read an insightful article on the subject of vulnerability and felt inspired to tap deeper into the vulnerable places within me. Moments after I finished reading the article, a gentlemen walked into the place I was working at the time. I had seen this gentleman a couple times before, but the reason I remembered him was because every time he came in I got a weird feeling. Not a bad feeling, just an unusual sensation. My intuition translated this energy that accompanied him as an older female energy that always walked with him. Being sensitive, I have had a number of occasions when I have been able to see or feel people who have crossed over, but it has been too inconsistent for me to feel confident translating. At the fear of sounding crazy, I had always kept it to myself and let curiosity kick me upon his departure. But this day, I had read that article. This day, nobody else was around. This day, my heart was going to pound out of my chest if I didn't say something, so I did. The man seemed a little more disheartened on this day so I asked him how he was. He said he was doing ok, unconvincingly, while sounding hopeful.

As my heart was pounding in my chest and I felt like I might vomit out of nervousness, I mustered up some courage and said, "At the risk of sounding crazy, every time you come in here, there's this strong female presence that comes with you. It's not you, it is an older woman, like a mom or grandmother, but I think it is your mom. She wants you to know that she's still here even though she's gone. Every time you're here she makes her presence known to me."

I was speaking really fast out of nervousness so I took a deep breath and the man stared at me for about thirty seconds and then told me that his mom had passed in 1997. He said they were really close and he was practically a (self-proclaimed) "momma's boy". He shared that he missed her very much and that Christmas was her favorite holiday, so it being around the holidays she had been on his mind a lot lately. That was the reason he was feeling a little down.

I reassured him that she was still with him often, especially when he was driving. He replied that he felt that was true; Recently he had fallen asleep at the wheel and he had no idea how he had gotten to his destination. He said he thought it must have been an angel. I told him it was his mom, but that she was similar to an angel in the way she was protecting him.

After about thirty minutes of enriching conversation, he left with a sincere thank you, to which I replied, "Thank you for allowing me to be vulnerable and share that with you. I often keep stuff like that to myself but I felt you should know." By the time he left, he had a smile on his face and a light about him.

This is when I realized the power of being vulnerable, the beauty in trusting in yourself and sharing your authentic self despite fear of judgment. There is something incredibly fulfilling about helping someone awaken to something much larger than themselves. Whether it is sharing a metaphysical experience like this one, or simply reflecting back someone's inner Divinity, it is a transformational and life changing experience. Vulnerability however, doesn't necessarily require a spiritual or religious component. It's not tied up in belief as much as it is a moment of speaking sincere truth even if your voice shakes.

Growing up in a Christian household, I was often taught that experiences like this were wrong, "of the devil", or a scam for frauds to get money from people. In my adult years, I have dismantled a lot of the illusion surrounding this, and harvested all the good I can from all religions to make peace with these experiences as a part of my reality. Fear of judgment is also the reason that I kept a lot of the conversations that I had with my father after his death to myself. I felt I would be misunderstood. Honestly my father helps me so much more now than he ever could have in the physical world. He, along with others, help me to understand the eternal life we all live. That heaven is not just a place we go when we die physically, but something attainable here and now. Death is not an end, but another beginning, just as many destinations are.

During adolescence and my early adult years I was so clouded by antidepressants and anti-anxiety medication that I never trusted my feelings or myself in general. It was not until about four years ago when I got off all of my meds that I realized that I am just very sensitive. I feel the world differently and I pick up on people's feelings very easily. This is also when I started receiving Divine messages with much more clarity. It was not that God wasn't always speaking to me; I just learned to listen better.

People often ask how I know when they are upset when I message them states away and have not spoken with them in months. Honestly, I don't know how. I have just learned to trust the things I feel. In my own self discovery, I have met others with similar gifts who also silence them or shut them off because they fear they will be seen as crazy, or because society sees it as taboo. "Crazy" has such a negative connotation to me because of my psychiatric history, but strangely enough I find that the people that are constantly checking up on their sanity are more sane than the rest. This is the art of perspective: some people see these experiences as a symptom of being crazy, while others see it as a gift.

We all possess special gifts that come with our authentic self.

Many people hide things like this because of the closed minded judgment and fear of others. Until recently, I did the same. Showing your true self may cause some people to leave your life out of fear or ignorance. The beauty is that you know that the people who stay love you for *all* that you are. They look deep into you and say, "Yes, I will love this person, unconditionally, for all they are and all they are not."

Spiritual experiences are not easily understood, nor are they comfortable all the time. Then again, when is staring at all of the parts of yourself and agreeing to let go of anything that does not serve your highest good comfortable? I do find that it makes genuine relationships more effortless, and peace and happiness much more plentiful. In accordance with the agreement *Don't take anything personally* from Don Miguel Ruiz's *The Four Agreements,* sharing yourself becomes easier when you realize judgmental reactions are not about you, but about the judge and an accumulation of their life experiences.

I am choosing to embrace my authentic self and all my gifts that come with it. I continue to share my love and light with the world, and most of all, embrace my vulnerability as a new found strength.

Vulnerability comes in all shapes and sizes. Although I shared this one unique experience that reflected the transformative power that vulnerability had in my life, vulnerability has its own special expression in your life. Vulnerability does not always come in the form of embracing a spiritual gift. Sometimes it can come in the form of telling the truth even if you feel there may be repercussions, getting up on a stage when you are afraid of public speaking, making a new friend, falling in love, making a choice to change your life even if you cannot see all of the pieces at the start, or asking for help when you have a need you can't fill on your own.

Vulnerability offers a personal invitation to make the choice between staying within the familiarity of your comfort zone, or to bravely offer ourselves to transformation and growth by stepping out of that comfort zone. Pride, fear and judgment are all qualities that keep us from embracing our vulnerability, which can be a source of strength and profound practice in faith.

Without perseverance through our vulnerable states, we begin to stagnate and only work with what we know. We adopt a dangerous and false sense of security in the comfort zone by denying ourselves the opportunity for growth. In contrast, making friends with our vulnerability opens doors where all we saw were walls.

A healthy perspective of vulnerability acknowledges that there may be a risk in exposing our insecurities but chooses to have faith in overcoming these fears. This is where vulnerability can become a super power. Unhealthy relationships with this aspect of ourselves will tell us that it is safer to stay small and stick with what we know. The ego is constantly negotiating the risk that a state of vulnerability can bring and steers us closer to growth or deeper into fear depending on the grip our ego has on us.

There is a tenderness associated with this. Admitting we do not know something offers an opportunity to learn something new. Admitting we need help offers an opportunity for someone to assist. Going on a first date not knowing if it will be a long term engagement or a one time event offers experience. When we listen to our intuition or trust our gut feelings, the threatening mask that vulnerability can wear seems less frightening. The risk of staying in the comfort zone stunts the growth of vitality and is ultimately a more threatening risk than stepping into the unknown.

Vulnerability has been a big theme in my life, as I am sure it has for many of you. When I was young, I wanted to be an actor. Every audition felt humiliating, but I kept challenging myself to overcome the fear until one day I began getting cast in plays. When I went to college, there was a sense of vulnerability in living in a new city, meeting new people, and receiving an education in a field I was not entirely sure I wanted to pursue a career in. Every new romantic relationship is a tender expression of vulnerability. We bring our past to the table and bare our wounds to examine if we are compatible with another. Crying is an expression of vulnerability. Apologies can feel vulnerable. Admitting you need help can be vulnerable. Quitting a traditional job to pursue your heart's desire is vulnerable.

Vulnerability is in no way a weakness. It can develop into one if we let it trap us in fear. If we act with our heart in a vulnerable state, we will expand our sense of strength farther than we knew imaginable. With this practice you will let vulnerability be a service to your spirit instead of a victim of your ego.

AN ATTITUDE OF GRATITUDE

"If the only prayer we ever say in our lives is "Thank you", that be enough"
-Meister Eckhart

The more we give, the more we have, but seldom do we understand that without first experiencing what it feels like to experience a perception of lack. At some point in time, we have all experienced what it feels like to not be recognized for a kind deed. With prolonged dynamics of abundance going unnoticed, we can feel that the receiving party is ungrateful and we feel unfulfilled in some way.

When we are grateful, we recognize blessings in every moment. We feel enriched with new eyes to see beauty in something we at one time overlooked, or perceive seemingly ordinary things as the extraordinary things that they really are. When we act in kindness with an agenda to be recognized or reciprocated, this is generally sparked by a sense of feeling unfulfilled in some way. We feel like we are not enough or do not have enough, and need validation for our actions in order to feel fulfilled. When we perform selfless acts of kindness, we already feel fulfilled, and the act is generally a compassionate sharing of that abundance with others. Our kindness does not define us, it becomes a living prayer. By activating our attitude of gratitude, we begin to resonate with a wholeness that never leaves us feeling depleted or empty. We have more than enough to share, and our passion for expressing our thanks to the world creates a ripple effect in the lives of others.

When we walk in gratitude, we awaken new eyes to the world around us. Gratitude magnetizes our perspective of what abundance already exists in our lives to help us to uncover and illuminate more hidden treasures around us. The world around us may not necessarily change at all to reveal this, it is the seer who changes.

Kindness and gratitude often walk hand in hand. When we feel grateful, it is difficult not to show it or desire to share it with others. When people are ungrateful, it is not likely that they aren't receiving kindness, but it is likely that they don't recognize a gift when it is given to them.

Gratitude is an effortless side effect of recognizing your wholeness. When we feel whole and fulfilled we can't help but feel grateful. By a simple gesture of "thank you" we signal to the Universe that we recognize the gift we received in this moment and also awaken our perspective to begin to see more gifts. Gratitude is a magnet for abundance and by recognizing all you have to be grateful for in the present moment, you align yourself with all the abundance that is waiting for you in the future.

An attitude of gratitude does not have to wait for a specific interaction or exchange to be practiced. In the present moment there are an infinite amount of things to be celebrated. If you opened your eyes this morning, this is a blessing. Breathing air filtered by the trees into your lungs is a repeating miracle. Whether it is your health, your home, your family, your pet, your loved one, food to nourish you, sun to warm you and give you vitamins, there are at least a few things you could cherish in any given moment. A busy mind may not recognize this, but with more appreciation, the mind becomes trained in noticing miracles in every moment.

It is difficult to be upset in traffic when your new awareness of gratitude has you focused on the fact that you have a vehicle or transportation, that the sun is shining, you have gas in your car and you have aspiration for a destination. When our awareness of gratitude is sleeping, the same event in traffic could be drawing our attention to how many people are on the streets, running late for work, the loud honks of horns, et cetera. Our outside world is influenced by our inner world of perspective. If we grew up in an environment where negative aspects of life were consistently highlighted for us, this is a more challenging perspective to adopt. By exercising our gratitude, we create an opportunity to shift our perspective into a whole new world of infinite abundance. Our gratitude does not stop with awareness of a kind deed or gift of convenience, like discovering a parking spot near your desired destination. Our gratitude graduates to a faith gratitude where we are thankful for things that have not even happened yet, or grateful for things that seem daunting now knowing that the gift is a buried treasure waiting to be revealed.

I began awakening to the transformative qualities of an attitude of gratitude in my early twenties. I was grateful for things before that time, and was thankful when people took time to say nice things or to give me gifts at holidays, but that was only a small part of gratitude. When I started awakening to all the abundance I had once overlooked, I felt like the richest woman in the world. This feeling only deepened with time. I became more present in conversation, counting the blessings conversation would bring. I would be in silent worship of my ability to hear, that communication was a daily miracle, that this person I was listening to had something they wished to share with me, be it an idea, a salutation, or a situation they sought advice for. I began to thank people often for simply Being. This practice brought more and more loving relationships into my life, and unexpectedly showered me with abundance in the form of gifts, kindness, money, and opportunities.

People that allow gratitude to saturate their being complete a circuit of reverence and appreciation. I have noticed this is not a requirement for a human to complete the circuit of appreciation. All sentient beings, trees, and animals offer a mirror of appreciation. This is perhaps easier to recognize in pets. For example, have you ever been grateful for your pet and in response, gave them a gift or food to show this affection? Most animals will respond in their own love language of gratitude represented in a variety of ways represented as joy, a lick translated as a kiss, or playful caress leaning against your leg.

All sentient beings feel our gratitude and respond with more things for us to shower appreciation for. It is not as common for us to thank a tree for its shade or the sun for shining, but when we do, we notice a subtle shift in our body that creates a lightness and expansive grace. Nature offers us many gifts that go unseen, but when we start noticing the rain washing the air, the trees filtering the air, plants feeding us, we expand into a greater sense of awareness that we are provided for more than we could ever realize.

The journey into a greater sense of gratitude only deepens. One never arrives in gratitude as a destination, but the sensation is relatable to a feeling of expansion in both our being and our capacity to love.

Recognizing abundance can be more challenging on days when we feel triggered by upsetting news or stressful events. It is human nature to look at something that is calling our attention. Be gentle to yourself during these days. It is not wrong to recognize where the world is suffering or where destruction is happening in the environment and humanity. This awareness sparks compassion, although it may not be our first emotional response.

Days of challenge are one of the best opportunities to practice gratitude. Your mind and body may be resistant, but if you can muster up the ability to grab a piece of paper and a pen, begin to make a list of all the things you can be grateful for despite the situation you are experiencing in that present moment. You may find the first things on your list to be a challenge to find, but don't be surprised when it becomes more effortless to find things to be grateful for as you watch the list grow.

Honoring the law of attraction, I will often write my gratitude for things that have not even happened yet on these days. If I am concerned with paying a certain bill, I will write how grateful I am that all my bills are paid and I even have extra money to save. If I am concerned about a relationship, I will find things to be grateful for in the relationship then I will add that I am thankful for the resolution of any conflicts and the growing sense of love in the partnership. If my health is challenging me, I will say that I am grateful for my healing. In fact, anytime that I am ill, I will never say that I am sick I will say, "I am healing." This helps me to be grateful for my health while eliminating any sense of judgment that my current status of health is wrong. This also works for global issues. Being grateful for world peace, health and wellness in all the nations, and a clean and thriving environment are powerful tools for aligning us with the solutions to heal what appears to be a broken world.

Gratitude can be expressed in a variety of ways. Some expressions are public displays of appreciation, others are a more personal sense of grace that is an intimate experience for only you. The joyful expression of gratitude is in the process, not attached to any outcome. The conscious act of gratitude is a transformational practice that will change your life and perspective forever.

FOOD AS THY MEDICINE

"Do the best you can until you know better
then when you know better, do better"
—Maya Angelou

Over the past twenty-six years, I have experienced many different perspectives in regards to my relationship with food. Once again, I am not a doctor or a nutritionist (although I have worked with many in the past ten years), yet I did have my own firsthand experience with obesity, and with healing into a state of overall well-being that offers a mind-body-spirit perspective on food relationships. Every body is different and although there are some collective truths on how to take care of it, eating is a personal and intimate thing and we must rely on our inner knowing of our unique style of care and nutrition.

I was diagnosed with obesity during my college years. When I saw this comment highlighted on my chart in the doctor's file I was surprised and mortified. I was 275 pounds at five feet, ten inches tall. I had no idea what that meant from a medical perspective and certainly had no idea that it classified me as obese.

I was blessed to always feel beautiful in my body. Growing up, I was often bullied for being "chubby". Children had a plethora of cruel names they would call me to try to make themselves feel superior, but I was blessed with a great mom who always told me the answer to conflict was to "kill it with kindness." I had peace in my heart about my physical body and generally looked at bullies compassionately, recognizing the suffering they carried underneath. I did not identify with the names they called me and I never saw myself as fat or obese; I felt beautiful. So, when I saw the word "obese" glaring at me from the file, I was shocked to see that it was associated with my body.

This shift in awareness invited me to understand health better and my brought awareness to my relationship with food. I had a friend in college who also struggled with her weight, and she invited me to join Jenny Craig with her, suggesting it would be a good way to support each other. Up until that point I really had no guidance on how to eat. I generally just ate what I wanted to when I was hungry. I grew up in a southern family where fried foods and comfort foods were regular menu items for dinner, and this was my frame of reference. Needless to say, when I started going to Jenny Craig for dietary counseling, they had their work cut out for them. Regardless of the changes you make, I would strongly suggest seeking the advice of a professional to monitor weight loss and any dramatic changes in eating styles.

The most valuable thing I learned during my two years of going to Jenny Craig was portion size, exercise, and how to really identify with my body if it was hungry or just craving something else for fulfillment. The food was not the most nutritious, but in comparison to what I was eating before, it was better and it gave me a great framework in which to build my own meals and eating lifestyle. I started recognizing when I was eating out of social activity, and how consciously preparing for events helped me not to stress eat or eat to feel included in the activity.

Food is everywhere and necessary for living. This is why it is one of the most unavoidable triggers when food is an addiction.

It can seem overwhelming when we are bombarded with commercials for deliciously marketed fast food, and it can be tempting just walking through the grocery store glancing at all the options.

Meal planning helped me tremendously with the temptation. If I planned my meals for the next four to five days and portioned them out respectfully, I knew I was provided for and did not get pulled into unexpected eating. It took discipline, and just like breaking any habit and creating a new one, you have to plan for prevention and have the will to stay true to the plan. Creating new activities to fill the space that my unhealthy habits use to occupy kept me active and excited. The first month was the most challenging, but it takes twenty-one days to create a new habit. From my experience, I found this to be a true and rewarding experience.

This new lifestyle change was not a restrictive diet; It was insight and direction into a better way of eating. Diets are a short term interest and not a self-loving practice. Diets are often sparked by a desire for quick results and include a lot of depriving yourself of what you want. Diets are temporary and leave us feeling temporarily satisfied with our results and continuously deprived.

The best weight loss trick is truly loving yourself as you are, to only desire healthier practices for your body. By loving yourself in your present condition, you are more gentle and loving in transitions. Just like when we love a child or a dear loved one, we want the best for them and start adjusting our life to meet that desire. When we look at our body in the same loving way, we celebrate it into a healthy progression, feeling fulfilled every moment along the way. Exercise is not punishment when we are doing it out of love. Rather it is celebratory and rewarding. We are not running away from our problems or our feelings of dissatisfaction, we are running into a newer, healthier version of ourselves. This is why, once again, it is all relative and it is within our perspective that we find our happiness.

Body health does not necessarily signify mental or emotional health, and vice versa. These parts work as a whole and they work best in balance with each other. Our thoughts about things transform our reality through the lens of perspective and directly effect our emotions. Our bodies tell us when something does not feel right and our emotions also impact our body. When we feel stressed, our body reacts to signal awareness in our mind. Some of the most physically fit people in the world can lack overall health by neglecting their emotional or mental well-being.

Working out and eating from a self-loving perspective provides more ease and encouragement than aspiring change through a self-loathing perspective. Knowing you deserve to feel good and healthy makes it easier to reward yourself with healthy decision making. Feeling beautiful from the start helped me to keep my lens of perspective clear and positive on the mission to be healthier and more fit, yet it was interesting to me how the more body conscious I felt, the more I lost weight.

After losing 100 pounds, I felt stronger and more confident than I had before. I felt driven and motivated to keep loving my body into a sustainable state of health. Oddly enough, however, I became a lot more self conscious of my body. When I was 275 pounds, I never questioned myself about wearing a bikini; I would wear one every time I would go to the pool and didn't ask myself if my body was "bikini ready". But the more body-focused I became, I asked myself questions like that. Ultimately, I realized that it was not the priority. Health is mind, body, and spirit, and some days our body needs the most attention, and sometimes it is our mind or our spirit. By dissolving a competitive or unhealthy comparative perspective, we free ourselves to be our own best version of ourselves. We only strive for competition with who we were yesterday, and aspire to be the best we can each day, knowing that our best will change from day to day.

Balancing the mental and physical parts of my wholeness, I recognized how health felt in my body. I listened intimately to how I felt each day and honored my body it didn't respond well to a certain food, or when it called for something else. I stopped drinking alcohol, although it was only something I did socially, and eliminated many unnecessarily chemicals from my diet. I adopted a Paleo eating lifestyle after I graduated from my season with Jenny Craig. A Paleo diet consists of primarily organic meats and vegetables, low sugar, small portions of fruit, no dairy and no grains. The cleaner I ate, the clearer I felt in my mind. I did not feel burdened by the emotions that had influenced my eating before, and I could distinguish my hunger needs and wants. I felt the healthiest and strongest I had in my whole life, and best of all, I felt I had a healthy relationship with self-love.

From this healthy plateau on the uphill climb, I recognized an increasing level of sensitivity to the world around me. Not a burdensome kind of sensitivity, but a feeling of interconnectedness with all things. My intuitive and empathic gifts were clear and evolving. Sometimes I could even hear people's thoughts and respond to questions before they were verbalized. With this sensitivity, I noticed my craving for more carbohydrates. When I felt open and sensitive, I wanted to shield myself to a comfortable state to process the world around me.

In the past, I would try to make myself "small" or unnoticed by self-medicating with food. Due to my art of modeling and using my body as an art form along with my use of my developing psychic gifts, I was receiving a lot of attention and it became a bit overwhelming. My sensitivities and my intuitive abilities were enhanced, and I was feeling very vulnerable to the sensations around and within me. So I began to eat more to comfort myself. Having experienced an unhealthy relationship with food before, I was aware of what I was doing this time around, but I was not sure how to stop. As stubborn as I can be, I don't like to ask for help. Ultimately, my intuition said, "Ask for help. Call upon the angels." The more I opened myself to the guidance of the angels, the more energized and eager to eat more healthy and conscious foods I became.

Many sensitive people are also emotional eaters. We tend to want to cushion what we feel by creating a barrier with something more dense. On a subconscious level, we want to shield and protect ourselves from feeling so intensely. Unconsciously, this can turn into emotional eating addiction, and when brought to a conscious perspective, food can be used as a healthy tool to feel more grounded when we are feeling unstable. Understanding why we feel sensitive and establishing our triggers keeps us in a healthy relationship with food. Instead of being manipulated by sensation, you can use food as a tool to create a more balanced perception of the energetic world around you.

It helps to shield in other ways that do not involve food so that you are not solely reliant on food to feel safe. There are a variety of ways to energetically shield and ground yourself so you don't feel whisked away by an energetic flux in the environment. Instead, we can stand in peaceful, centered presence and experience emotions like the sky experiences clouds.

Visualization is one of my favorite ways to shield. Much like visualization for manifestation, you may feel silly when you first try this. One of great qualities of visualization is that nobody else has to know you're doing it, yet you can feel the difference it makes.

I like to do this every morning before I open my door to go out of my house. While I am still in bed, I will image a white light in the center of my chest that expands to surround me like a large bubble. I fill this light with whatever color feels safe and relaxing to me in that moment. On days when I am feeling attacked energetically by somebody else, I visualize mirrors or reflective material on the outside of my bubble. When I do this, I set the intention that this mirror will protect me from any ill-intention and reflect the intentions of others with three times the amplification to create awareness of their energy. I also add that I would like to serve the highest good of all involved.

When you try this, go about your day and pay attention to your experiences. I have had clients return to me amazed by the results. Some people have even said that when they did this, especially at work, the people that used to pick on them or cause conflict in their day stopped interacting with them completely. Some also said that people who were historically bullies to them began to be more kind. Other clients have mentioned that when they tried this in extremely stressful environments, they noticed that they did not adopt the feelings or chaos of those in the environment, but were able to maintain a more peaceful disposition.

Another fun way to shield is to imagine standing in a vertical tanning bed which surrounds you completely. Imagine putting a seal on the bottom of the cylinder, and fill the space with light from the top. Pulling in white light from the crown of your head also activates your crown chakra which is the energy center of your Source (God) wisdom on your body. There are seven chakras aligned vertically in the body that are energy centers for areas of the body that help us to stay balanced, strong, and healthy in the areas associated with each one. Once you do this, imagine placing a seal to close off the area above your head and then go about your day and experience the results. Check in with this feeling that you have in the moment you create this safety shield and feel free to refresh it throughout the day. Our thoughts are powerful and shape our reality. You can design these shielding practices any way you wish that suits your life. The important part is that it feels good to you and that you feel safe and grounded as you go about your day. A simple mantra you can use throughout your day is, "I am protected, I am safe." Anytime you feel uneasy, restless, unsafe, or threatened, say these words aloud until you find yourself feeling centered and safe. I often use this mantra while driving in heavy traffic.

You may be asking yourself, "what does this have to do with food?" When we don't feel safe in our body, we try to cushion our feelings with other things. This is how we develop vices. For some the vice is sex, drugs, or alcohol, and for many people it is food. The more we bring awareness to our bodies and what we are feeling, the better we can understand our triggers and create new practices for fulfilling the needs without a vice.

The more sensitive you are, the more you feel, and many times the more we feel unpleasant things, the more we try to turn them off. Practicing the visualization of shielding gives us another tool that is healthier to our bodies than binge eating, and allows us to observe our environment without taking it on personally.

What happens when we do all of this but we are still feeling anger, sadness, discomfort and it seems to be coming from the inside out? This directs our attention to what it is we are actually feeding ourselves and digesting and integrating into our body. Many naturally occurring chemicals and hormones in our body can influence emotional changes within our bodies. Some may require a medical professional's assistance. Another way to gain insight on energetic and chemical influences is to take a closer look at what we are actually consuming.

One summer, I was becoming easily agitated. Seldom do I feel anger, so I knew something was needing my attention and something needed to change. Many months prior to this, I was at a used book store and saw a book glowing (things appear to glow in my perception of reality when Spirit is trying to get my attention). The book was entitled *Anger* by Thich Nhat Hanh. At the time that I bought the book, I assumed I was buying it because I would need to gift it to someone else. Little did I know that months later, this book would come into my awareness again as it glowed from my bookshelf during a time of agitated emotions.

To my surprise, the whole first chapter was about food. It discussed energy and food consumption and the potential for suffering to carry on energetically from source of food to consumer. "Wow!" I thought, this made so much sense. This planted a seed in my mind, but it was not until a couple months later would I understand how to incorporate this into my own life.

In mid-July, I went to a dear friend's house. She has this beautiful porch, lush with green vegetation and all of the birds seem to love being there. We had a certain time of day, an hour before sunset, that we called Cardinal Hour. Cardinal Hour is the time of day that all the cardinals come to feed and bathe in her back yard.

On this particular day, I had stopped by PDQ. PDQ is a fast food establishment specializing in fried chicken. On the way to Cardinal Hour I had picked up some chicken tenders for dinner. I spent the afternoon bird watching. I watched them as they played, fed, and mated. I would laugh in amusement at how they related to one another and communicated in song. Afterward, I went to eat dinner and as I began to chew a seemingly delicious chicken tender, my mouth did not taste it in the same way as it had in the past. I began realizing how the experience had shifted my perception and, with that, had begun to enlighten the cells in my body. How is a cardinal that I became so delighted by so different from a chicken that I decided to eat for dinner? It wasn't. My awareness expanded into great compassion for animals and how ignorant I had been to their suffering up until this point. Radiating my humble apology from my heart center, I immediately forgave myself and everyone else whose awareness was yet to be expanded on this topic. I decided to, once again, change my lifestyle right then and there.

I had already been eating clean on my Paleo lifestyle. I had eliminated unnecessary chemicals and added hormones, but what I did not consider was the source of my meat, an animal's life, to hold the suffering in its body that I would eventually integrate into mine through food. This added layer of awareness is where I made the choice to adopt a cruelty-free eating lifestyle and to eliminate harsh chemicals and violent energy from entering my body. Not only did I feel rewarded by feeling healthier physically and mentally, I found an increased level of compassion for myself and other sentient beings. I feel radiant most days and my intuitive gifts continue to get clearer the cleaner I eat.

Over time, what I found to be the most beneficial tool in my journey of healthy eating was to be present with every meal. Even if I am eating just a snack, it is so important to take the time to eat a meal without too many distractions. I have adopted a presence practice with my food where I take a moment before I eat anything and think of the intention I am using in eating the meal. Is it fulfilling hunger? Do I wish for easy digestion? Is the desire to have more energy or nutrition? Whatever the intention may be, I take a moment to mentally infuse my food, pause in gratitude, and then consume.

Being present with my food allows me to enjoy the taste so

much more and helps me to gauge when I am full and I have had enough. It is a practice I have found to be a consistently rewarding experience in my relationship with food. It is also beneficial to dedicate the moment you are eating to make eating the priority. It is easy to want to multitask or become distracted, but if you pace yourself and focus on the experience at present: eating, that alone can help you to lose weight, hear your body, provide ease with digestion, and give you a new found appreciation for food in general.

Listen to your body. It is the finest divination tool you could possess. Our bodies are constantly talking and signaling our needs. From hunger to sickness, to strength and health, to fight or flight response, to gut reactions and emotions, we are in communication with our body. The more we become in tune with our vessel the more we tap into the consciousness surrounding it.

Have you ever gotten that feeling in your gut that something was not right? Not an actual digestive sensation, but a physical reaction to a situation, person, or environment. Our bodies are designed to protect us and keep us informed. Our job is to listen. Through meditation, we can sit in alert yet passive awareness, observing the traffic of our thoughts in the mind and the sensations in the body. We not only create more peace in our minds with a meditation practice, but can also heal the body and transform unhealthy habits from this state of Being. Here, it is important to note that the more clear you get in your thoughts, the more you are able to understand the messages your unique body is giving you to achieve maximum potential health and healing. Not every body is the same, but every body talks.

RELATIONSHIPS

*"The world is a reflection of ourselves. If we don't like what we see, it
doesn't help to break the mirror."*
—Deepak Chopra

A former coworker once asked me if the reason I am so happy
and glow like I do is because I am in love. Then I smiled and
said, "Of course I am in love! That's all there is." Love is
unconditional. Relationships, however, are very conditional.

The good thing about life is that it is always changing. One of
the challenging aspects of life is that it is always changing. This
is why change is a more difficult concept to accept. Much like
the cycles of life, all relationships are fluid. Some are a little
more difficult to let go of, but nonetheless they go. Thus the
impermanence of life in the human form. Discovering how to
graciously let go of what no longer is meant for us is the key to
more peaceful relationships. Our resistance and ego-driven
agendas perpetuates the conflicts that many of us have
experienced in the dating scene. We can jump from one
relationship to another and experience similar dynamics, just
with different people.

In the cycle of relationships and being single, it is important to
learn how to be alone. It is even more important to learn to love

the person you are alone with. When you need to be around others constantly, ask yourself why. Are you hiding there? Are you hiding from your stillness? What will you find there?

Relationships and human interaction are significant parts of our life journey which enable the growth and development of our soul family. These opportunities to partake in community should not be neglected either. The balance between the two is the sweet spot for the soul. There is healing in solitude and there is healing in community.

The Relationship with God and Ourselves

Within relationships, it is easy to hide from ourselves. With others we can feel desired, liked, loved, and many people use that to establish their worth and happiness. But if you can't feel complete, comfortable, and whole by yourself, a vital connection is missing: the connection to your Higher Self. What happens if your romance, family, friendship dissolves? Do you run to the next validation zone in the arms of another? It is easy to fall to the temptation of the validation from others, but total acceptance of your own true self is key to inner peace and unconditional self-love. Our relationship with God and ourselves is the most significant relationship in our lives. At times it is important to strengthen the relationship with yourself and the Universe, and acknowledging this will allow gratitude to fill space where you once experienced loneliness. To strengthen our relationship with ourselves and Spirit, we must be self-aware, not self-judging. Witness yourself on the scales of these two worlds. Only you know the sweet spot for your soul.

The reason why this section is first in this chapter is because this is the relationship that is often neglected and begins to reflect in all of our other various relationships. I spent twenty-three years failing to understand the significance of this. Admittedly, for many of those years I didn't even realize that I could have a relationship with myself. When we just go through the motions of life, we miss out on self-nurturing, self-discovery, and self-love. When we awaken to the realization that our relationship with ourselves and our relationship with our Higher Self is the most important relationship we can have, we act in a way congruent to that discovery and live a lifelong romance with ourselves.

If you don't fill yourself up first, you will never find complete fulfillment in a partner. You must discover what your truth is and learn to love yourself for all you are and all you are not. In total acceptance of yourself, you are able to love yourself unconditionally. Nobody can make you feel less than what you are, and the presence or absence of someone else in your life cannot take away your truth or self-love.

The deeper we go in our self discovery we awaken the Divinity within. God and you are not two separate things. We (all that is) is God, and God is us. It's as if everything you see are cells in the body of God, and creation and experience are thoughts in the mind of God. When you find God within, you can't help but to fall madly in love and transform into a beacon of love yourself. Recognizing the Great Spirit within cleanses the perspective of self reflection. You are complete, you are whole, you are innately abundant, and you are loved. No one can change that except you and your own perspective distancing you from the vision of Divine truth.

I spent a couple of years basking in the glory of being s'

loving me. I would romance myself and treat myself as I desired a future lover to treat me. I took myself out for fun dates and candlelit dinners. I made myself bubble baths with salts and essential oils. I would take the time to give myself foot massages and facials while always pondering how I could express love to myself more. This is not selfish or arrogant, this is self care. Self care can vary person to person, but you know you're experiencing it when you feel nurtured by yourself. When we feel we deserve great love, we are open and receptive to it in all ways. When we act "as if", we create a reality that ripples out through the Universe that this is what we wish to attract.

During this time, I was able to recognize that when people really wanted to date me, they would make a profound effort to do so. It wasn't necessary to give out my number or make it convenient to potential partners. If they wanted to be around me they would make it happen with little to no effort on my part. Treating myself in a loving way was an inviting quality to have and made people want to come into my love orbit. Not relying on others to fill my love cup, I surrendered any desire to make someone anything other than what they were. By fully accepting myself, I would accept others as they were and discern whether I wanted them in my life. I valued how I spent my time and treasured my solitude in which I could commune with Spirit through meditation and other various practices.

We teach people how to treat us. If we are too busy looking outside of ourselves to determine who we are and what we want, people will not know how to treat us any better than we treat ourselves. If we treat ourselves badly or neglect ourselves, this is our demonstration of how we want to be loved. If we speak to ourselves lovingly and treat ourselves with romance, this is what we will attract. It all begins with you. You, your soul, are consistent figures in your life while everything else is temporary. Whether it is a break-up, a graduation, a death, a birth, relationships change and so we cannot build our foundation of love on these grounds. We must build our foundation within our personal temple of love, the home of our Being. Only then can the structure hold all of our other relationships to come.

Self-love is a challenging expression for some people. To utter the words, "I love myself," can feel foreign or strange at first. Some people would even consider belittling a spirit in the discovery of self-love and dismiss it as arrogance. Self-love and arrogance are not compatible. Self love, true self-love is the unconditional kind. Self love is not only a birthright, but a reward I feel I have won against my ego. I spent years in the battlefield of belittling myself and feeling unworthy. I climbed mountains in my psyche, invaded fortresses within, fought dragons and shadowy reflections, and broke down and got back up. I played victim as though it was someone else who was keeping me from me until one day, feeling broken, defeated, like a puzzle with too many pieces and not enough clues, it happened. Like a flower that bloomed in the garden of my heart when I wasn't looking, I finally found it.

Since then it has been a love fest. Bare-faced, no mask, I love this woman. All dolled up, I love her the same. I love her for the light within and her fire to express herself through her variety of art. Her hair, makeup, fashion do not define her. But neither does her bare naked body. It is her bare naked soul that makes this light glow bright. It is the puzzle unfinished, yet complete, that makes my heart skip beats. I love her compassion to help others and raise others up because she knows what it is like to be put down. I love the galaxies slowly spinning in her eyes. I love the mystery.

When I say, "I love myself," it has depth to which no earthly ocean can compare. My right, my reward, my celebration, my gift. It is something I wish I could bottle and give to all the broken hearted people, but then I know victory would not taste so sweet for the beloved as self-discovery. You forget yourself, you find yourself, then you see that reflection in others. When you discover self-love, loving others is an inevitable side effect. I love the woman I have become, and I love the soul I finely recognized within.

I sincerely encourage you to awaken the love that is within and dare to go deep. This love cannot be taken from you and you will only want to share what you find there.

Relationships with Romantic Partners

The first and most important step in a relationship with another person (after, of course, learning to love yourself) is knowing that you cannot change another person. People change when they want to change. All that you can do is accept them completely as they are and provide a loving environment to nurture and encourage them.

I have been in a handful of serious relationships, and on a number of dates where the other person or myself would look to each other to fill a void where we did not love ourselves. We only accept the love we think we deserve, and without a healthy relationship with ourselves there is often a conflict where one person doesn't feel like they are getting enough. A sense of lack can create a lot of problems in relationships and often times the lack is not a material thing it is something that goes overlooked and unnoticed because it begins with the individual.

Until I had my ah-ha moment in the world of relationships, I spent twenty-three years blindly accepting disrespect, desperately working to make relationships "perfect", and putting far more effort and emotion into relationships than some of my apathetic partners. I was in the dynamic of compensating my feelings for my partners' lack of emotional reciprocation. I was unsure of myself and needed a partner to validate that I was worthy of love, and I chased affection every chance I got. I don't believe people can be lost, but if there was ever a time in my life where I could have been, it was then.

In my experience, after I established a healthy relationship with me, I no longer seemed to attract relationships that were otherwise. In the moment of realization, I promised myself that from that day forth I would not allow the disrespect that I had endured before. I pledged to myself that I would never let another person make me feel like I was not special or unworthy of love. I learned how to forgive all the partners and experiences I had that led me to this clarity and said a prayer for all of them to awaken to the same love that I now knew so that they could have healthier relationships, too.

A tool I found very helpful in forgiving a partner and healing from a relationship is to write a note to that partner that you will never give to them. Also, write a letter as you would imagine they would write as an apology to you. We don't necessarily need apologies from someone to forgive them, but it often helps. Many people never receive those apologies, or if they do, it is much later in life. Here is an example of a letter I once wrote from the perspective of my ex-lover and it was tremendously helped in my healing. I encourage you to use this to inspire your own personalized letter of healing and forgiveness.

Samantha,

I know I have hurt you. I know I have lied. I know that I made things seem like they were promising to only turn around and tell all my friends that you were not important to me. I am not sure why I do these things. I am afraid to feel. You were the first person I felt something for in a long time and this scared me. You have been so supportive, kind, and loving and I guess one of the reasons I started backing away is that I didn't think I deserved that. I know I treated you badly and you were always just trying to help. I want you to know that I am sorry. You did not deserve everything I put you through and all the hurtful things I have said. I guess I am still trying to figure out what I want in life. I want to pursue my careers and work on my passions and I felt that you distracted me from this. I didn't want to be responsible for your emotions. I have told you before, but I'll say it again, you are beautiful. You're smart, independent, brave, and responsible. Although this is intimidating to me, I admire and appreciate all of the qualities in you. At this point in my life, I am loving you in the best way I know how and you don't deserve to be treated this way. You deserve someone that can hold all of you for all that you are. I know whoever that lucky person is, they will be grateful to have you. I am truly sorry. I appreciate all you did for me. I wish you the best.

Sincerely, The Anonymous Ex

Of course my ex-partner did not write this, but this is the compassionate apology that I deserved and that I felt I needed in order to forgive and move on. I realized while writing this that we often surrender our power to a person by making our personal peace conditional on something only someone else can give us. We must give to ourselves what we need to be healthy, happy, and loved.

I once asked myself, "Why do I attract all the broken birds?" In humble self-discovery I found my answer. We engage in relationships that are a reflection of our subconscious pain. If we are conscious we disengage from unhealthy relationships. We establish healthy boundaries. Our dynamic with our partner is merely a reflection of ourselves. A canvas to paint and project our life experience upon. Relationships are for healing. We are whole within ourselves, but our communion with others strips layers of our ego, our false self, and reveals what is truly underneath. This is the healing power of relationships. If two people are participating in a relationship from an awakened state of consciousness, the healing happens in a very compassionate way. There is an understanding and big picture perspective from the level of Spirit. When two people are pursuing a relationship from an unconscious level (lacking self-awareness), the pain can rage on indefinitely, projecting the struggles back and forth between two psyches.

When aspiring to a healthy partnership, knowing what we want in a partner is half the battle. However, staying true to our desires and not accepting less is where many people fall short. Not every partner is prince charming or a princess, but luckily not everyone is looking for that. Many of us have basic standards in a partner, and oftentimes we sacrifice our standards for convenience and instant gratification. When we fill ourselves up with self-love first, we tend to not behave like an addict when we engage with potential partners. We can healthily observe if a partner is compatible with us and discern if they want similar things we do in life. If we don't know what we want or where we want to go, we will rely on someone else to answer that for us which can later make us resentful and put a lot of pressure on our partner.

Developmental compatibility is another valuable asset in a relationship. True success in relationships is not only reliant on love but on developing at similar paces throughout different stages in life. It is not uncommon for people to meet on an equal playing field with similar endeavors only to later have one partner undergo a valiant growth spurt, leaving the other partner to catch up. This is not to say that one partner can't be extremely successful and the other partner have a humble nature. It simply means that both partners have to be growing or developing similarly to still be able to relate and grow in the same direction.

Envision two trees growing side by side, their branches eager to meet and intertwine, and together they grow tall and strong. This is how a healthy relationship can be described. An unhealthy relationship is similar to one partner being represented by a strong tree and another partner climbing the tree and holding on as the tree ascends. Dynamics such as these can create codependency if enabled. In healthy relationships, two partners exist as wholeness individually and unify to grow, create, and experience romantic love in another being. When we start cutting corners in relationships, things that were somewhat tolerable at one time can develop into a loathsome debilitation of the relationship. Finding conscious ways to check in with yourself and monitor your true desires in comparison to what you are tolerating is important in maintaining a healthy, developing relationship.

Establish a way to hold space for another to heal and grow without hindering your goals or creating a dynamic of codependency. "Holding space" is a term I use to describe the non-judgmental, loving, compassionate space we hold by staying present for someone who is going through a difficult situation. We can hold space for ourselves, friends, family, romantic partners, and even strangers. We hold this space without creating an agenda or making things personal. This allows the person being energetically held to have the freedom and sense of security to process emotions and heal.

Communication is vital for growth and development, but we must first identify what we are wishing to communicate. Trusting in a relationship and making yourself vulnerable to the unknown potential outcomes is a courageous quality. Vulnerability in relationships is a strength to be recognized especially in regards to communication. By identifying what we need in life and in a partner, we can transparently communicate our needs with more likelihood that they will be provided for. Communication with a pure desire to share, heal, and empower one another is valuable. Many times in a relationship, partners can try to manipulate or satisfy a personal agenda with their communication. In selfishness, borders are made that cut off the flow of love and Spirit that effortlessly flow with pure intention.

How often has it happened that your partner has had a bad day at work and comes home carrying a hostile energy, speaking aggressively, insultingly, or even apathetically? Just like I mentioned in the section about anger, by being conscious to our own truth, we are less likely to adopt chaos from another. In relationships, not exclusively romantic partnerships, we tend to act as mirrors when we fall victim to someone else's emotions. When we become clear in the relationship with ourselves, it is easier to act as a window to Spirit than to react in the same energy that is being directed toward us from another. If a person cannot healthily communicate, the relationship is destined to have increased levels of conflict. It is unlikely that we will always take an enlightened approach to someone yelling at us, but if we provide space for healthy communication to happen, we can quickly dissolve most misunderstandings.

Some relationships rely on drama or conflict to create a sense of passion that causes the relationship to only exist in polarity. These relationships are not only unhealthy, they can be draining and lack the genuine foundation of love. Lust has a powerfully intoxicating effect. Much like a drug, lust survives on intensity and chasing thrills. There are sensations of withdrawal that can occur in lust-based relationships which resonate a sense of lack within us. Lust can be a powerful sexual device for a healthy relationship, and create passion to enhance physical acts of love. Lust without love cannot survive long term. This is why many psychologists say that couples that get married within two years of dating are likely to have more challenges or divorce because the lust dynamic often wanes after about two years. Lust is not necessarily good or bad, but it is not a solid foundation for a sustainable healthy relationship.

Traits associated with healthy relationships are integrity, accountability, loyalty, trust, clear communication, compassion, service, developmental compatibility, and love. We must acknowledge people to be who they show us they are as opposed to just trusting how people describe themselves . True love exists on total acceptance of the present moment, not conditional on someone developing into our standard of what we deem as lovable. When acting in love, we can also surrender to the natural flow of waxing and waning of the lifetime of relationships. True love gives us a compassionate eye to know to let go. This compassionate eye will help you recognize when you want someone's peace and happiness more than you want to have your way. This sacrifice does not even feel like sacrifice because your love is so strong and unconditional that you are able to gracefully let go of what is no longer meant to be in your life. The physical separateness from this person may sting your ego, but your truth is much more powerful than the sting.

To love someone is to set them free. Trusting what remains to be the omnipresent truth. Loving unconditionally does not mean that relationships are unconditional. Relationships require nurturing. They require developmental compatibility. Two people must grow together at similar paces or they will grow farther and farther apart. To love yourself unconditionally is to set yourself free. How can you be in a union and be free? Free yourself from expectation. Gracefully let go of what is no longer meant for you. Surrender to love and embrace what remains. Trying to control radiates a message to the Universe that you think you have a better plan than the one that is unfolding before you. By surrendering, there is grace and peace. What is meant for you will never miss you on your path. By relinquishing control, you align yourself with the Divine flow of the Universe. This does not mean to be passive, however. This state of being is in constant agreement with what life brings.

When we identify ourselves by our relationships, we allow ego to rush us into dynamics, and we tend to turn deaf to our inner voice. Your soul mate is just as eager to find you as you are them. Soul mate is a tricky term because it tends to lead people to believe we only have one. There is a sense of desperation surrounding the desire to find the perfect one as if there is only one person for us. The truth is, we have multiple soul mates. Not all of our soul mates are a happily-ever-after fairytale partnerships. When we pick our soul mates before incarnating

87

here, we choose them because they are familiar beings from previous incarnations that desire to help us to know love more deeply. It is comparable to having a set of co-workers that agree to work with you on multiple projects, or a cast of actors that act in different plays performing in similar roles. The goal is to remember the love that we are, and this does not always happen easily and effortlessly. Many our soul mates are chosen because they will help us grow and gain experience through challenges. When we have learned the lesson, these soul mates tend to exit our lives in one form or another to allow another soul mate to enter. There are times where your soul mate is your lover and long-term mate.

Soul mates are not to be confused with twin flames. Twin flame is a term used to describe a person or soul that is the closest to your soul vibration as your own. The term twin is in reference to the similarity of souls that is comparable to the biological similarities to two identical twins. The experience of communing with your twin flame in your lifetime is often described as the closest physical experience we can have that is relatable to the communion of God. Through some of my intuitive sessions with clients, I discovered that not all humans on this planet have a twin flame that is incarnated in the same lifetime as them. Some of us make agreements, similar to spiritual contracts, with our twin flame that they will guide us through a particular incarnation from the other side of the veil like a spirit guide. The love is just as genuine as if you did spend a lifetime together, but for these people, they experience the love in a different way and wait to reunite after their specific incarnation.

Whether or not your twin flame is incarnated with you in this lifetime should not keep you from experiencing all of the wonderful things relationships have to offer. You can still experience love, happiness, growth, and a relationship of longevity even if your partner is not your twin flame or soul mate.

After we experience sensations associated with heartbreak, many of us are hesitant to open ourselves to a relationship again. It is important to note that although our relationships have conditions and expiration dates, the love we share is eternal. Conditional love is limited, but unconditional love is boundless and infinite. Love withstands all earthly dynamics as well as time, dimension, and form. Love is all there is. Being afraid of commitment, feelings, or getting emotionally wounded again only distances you further from the opportunity of romantic partnership and the healing capacity relationships can bring. It is healthy to take time to rest, heal, recharge, and reevaluate, but do not let fear be a prison of loneliness when there is so much to share with a loved one. To feel deeply is to engage in a human experience. This is the secret to life's purpose.

Relationships with Friends and Family

Many of the practices of love, non-attachment, acceptance, and compassion that I discussed in the section about romantic partners can also be practiced in the context of family and friends. Most everyone has a group of people, or maybe just a single person, that they can call family. Not all family is blood related. Some family is adopted either by choice or during infancy. Family can be a child and a single parent or extensive and communal. The Hawaiian word *Ohana* means family and refers to not only the bonds made by genetics, but the extensive family that is community. In Disney's animated movie *Lilo and Stich,* Lilo recites the phrase, "Ohana means family," and then follows up with, "and family means nobody is left behind or forgotten." This is such a precious translation of what families represent.

Not everyone has had an ideal upbringing. Some people may have left their birth families, fleeing abusive or unhealthy situations. Some may be adopted and never have known their birth family. Some may have stayed with their family until the legal age of eighteen and never turned back. Some may hold their families sacred and honor them for life. There are many variations but the term family is relatable to one degree or another.

A unique quality of families is that our relationships change over time with the evolution of needs, responsibilities in roles, age, and caretaking. Upon birth, we are cared for and nurtured as vulnerable infants. As we mature and grow with age, our relationship with our parents evolve as we experience life in different ways. When our parents grow older, we often become their caretaker until the end of their life here on Earth.

Familial relationships tend to be the longest relationships in our lives, regardless of how close we are to our family. We see firsthand our loved ones transform, evolve, and experience life from various physical, emotional, and mental stages. Whether we like it our not, our parents know intimate aspects of our growth and childhood that is a reference point for all we grow up to do in our adult lives.

Our family ties are not severed upon earthly death. In fact, sometimes the parent or sibling that you did not necessarily get along with can help you more after their life in the physical world is over. I was a daddy's girl from birth and craved a perfect father-daughter relationship with him. My dad was a workaholic and an alcoholic, so when he wasn't working, he was often drinking. There were various times in my childhood when we would vacation as a family, and those were my most treasured times with my family. No matter how much I wanted to spend time with my father, he often felt overwhelmed by work and did not want to spend his off-work hours playing with or entertaining my brother and I. My dad was a very loved man and very successful at his job. He voiced that he provided for us with a roof over our heads, food on the table, and financially, and he did not understand my bothersome requests for quality time.

A couple of years before he died, I had the realization that my dad was my father but he was also his own person. In my adult life I did not need him to be the father I needed him to be when I was a child. I learned to forgive him for the ways that I once thought he had failed me, and realized that just because he did not love me the way I wanted to be loved did not mean he didn't love me with all he had. During the last two years of his life we healed my childhood wounds, but we still were not very close. Only after he died did I find profound clarity in our parent-child relationship.

On a soul level, I needed my father to be exactly as he was. From that dynamic, I learned to be independent, self-sufficient, compassionate, and learned to speak a variety of love languages, recognizing my father's total disregard. I had my father's leadership qualities and his social skills. I learned from my father how I needed to learn, not necesarily how I wanted to learn.

At 53, my father died of a sudden cardiac arrest in his sleep. Thankfully for my intuitive gifts, when my father passed, he visited me almost immediately. There were not many words at first but there was a clear recognition and understanding of our roles in each other's lives. I could also see he was not in any pain; He was smiling and even laughing! Even in spirit, my father is protective, supportive, and can help me in many more ways than he could in his physical body. In spirit, the love between family members is pure and not as situational or jaded.

Even though this is a personal story that is not relatable to everyone, it is an anecdote that reflects the timelessness of family and the love we share. We are blessed to have good relationships with our family when they are alive, but the potential to heal does not stop in death.

For relationships with our family members that are challenging, the tools I mentioned in the previous section regarding clear communication, making space, total acceptance, and freeing yourself also apply here. We should never stay in a situation that is abusive or unhealthy to us, but as children, we sometimes do not have a choice. We are more limited and vulnerable as children than in our adult lives, but as adults we must find ways to make conscious, healthy decisions in our relationships. There are a lot of traditional obligatory concepts associated with family relationships. We have a false sense of entrapment in social gatherings, and, depending on how we were raised, we either voice our opinions about it or sit in silent suffering.

I adore my family, however, in my adult life I have become much more brave in transparently communicating my likes and dislikes in regards to family gatherings. At first there was some resistance on the receiving end, but I learned the more that I respected myself and stood in my truth, the more I taught people how to treat me and the more they learned to respect my input. Some relatives are not going to be as conscious in receiving your requests, but if you speak from the heart, eventually the emotional transfer will translate into understanding.

Friendships are similar to family relationships but have even more variety of dynamics. Some friends are for a season, others are for a reason, and in rare cases, we hold some friendships for a lifetime. Friendships can be situational or based on convenience. These relationships usually exist in the context of school, work, or mutual friends. We have friends that we also have created soul contracts with that will be a part of our challenging lessons, and console us during heartache. It is hard to be everybody's best friend, but a little bit of compassion goes a long way. Most of the time I feel that even strangers are just friends we have not met yet.

Everyday we engage with others. People arrive with all sorts of history and unique personality traits. Although I cannot know a person fully within these fleeting interactions, I remind myself that it takes no prior knowledge to be kind. Never underestimate someone's capacity to suffer, but also never underestimate your capacity to love them into a healthier state of being. I generally ask myself how I would want or need to be loved during a time of heartache, pain, or healing. Then I do my best to arrive with that level of understanding and compassion toward others. There is no need to figure someone out in order to simply be understanding. When the current reality is one of suffering for this soul sibling, love them back to happiness and recovery.

Surround yourself with people who encourage you and love you. Friendship is not a competition but a joining of two people walking a similar path for an unknown period of time. I honor the impermanence of friendships because the ebb and flow is what allows us the opportunity to meet so many friends in our lifetime. If we always saturated our time with the same people we went to kindergarten with, we would not experience all the variety of people life has to offer. Bless your friendships as they come in closeness, and with the same gratitude, bless them as they go. Relationships do not have to end in conflict, and friendships don't necessarily have to end at all, but our human mind often makes conflict out of such cycles of relationships. When we resist the natural flow, we create our own suffering where otherwise relationships could organically wane without any cause for hardship.

There is a richness in the relationships of family, friends, and community. When counting wealth in means of love, your life will always prove abundant. Gratitude is a powerful tool in uniting people. When we focus in the good of our loved ones, we will see more of that goodness. When we breakdown or criticize our brothers and sisters, we separate ourselves farther from oneness. Be loving and kind, and you will forever be a magnet to positive, loving relationships.

Relationship with Humanity and Planet Earth

There is a beautiful saying in Native American culture: *Mitakuye Oyasin*, which translates to, "We are all related." I love this phrase because it is a beautiful reminder that we are all family here. We are one big soul family where some of us our bonded in blood, and many of us are bonded in friendship that is a relationship that transcends genetics and blood. When we start to acknowledge all of humanity as our brothers, our sisters, our elders, and our loved ones, we dissolve the separateness of race and cultural upbringing and unite on the level of love. We heal the *us versus them* mentality and we see the light that exists within all of us reflected throughout humanity.

Peace begins with us. When we experience peace within, it ripples out into the world and transforms it. Sometimes it takes years to see, but nonetheless, transformation is happening. Peace and chaos do not just effect the people of humanity. They affect the planet that we live on. At the 2nd Annual Meditation for Compassion, Deepak Chopra reflected on this by opening our eyes to see that we are not separate from the planet. He explained that the trees of Earth are our lungs, the rivers and streams are our circulation, and the Earth is our body. Some cultures have recognized this since the beginning of civilization, but over time we have grown further from this truth. We are awakening to this reality again, as a human race, and we are starting to see the ways that our personal peace can transform the world. The same can be said for the inverse. Our personal chaos or disharmony can create war and disease throughout the world.

We are at a point in time when the people of the planet are slowly but surely waking up to their responsibility to maintain a sustaining planet. With self-awareness, we can turn within to make profound results externally, healing our world. Within this human family is the salvation we seek. We have an incredible ability to heal what seems to be so far lost. It can feel overwhelming to hold this responsibility when we just seek to change the world outside of us and we do not feel like we can ever keep up. Shifting the perspective within, we see that peace is possible. We must first know what that feels like within us before we can create it outside of us.

Acts of service and kindness are another way to contribute to the healing of humanity. You don't have to give a lot to make a big difference. Honoring the flow of giving and receiving, you will always find you have more when you give. Whether you give of your time, your money, your food, or your love, it is all needed and it helps. Sometimes a simple gesture of opening the door for someone, giving someone a ride, or paying a nice compliment creates a profound change in someone's day. I personally feel that a smile can save someone's life. With a history of depression, there were many times when I felt like life was not worth living and a simple smile kept me going to see another day.

Some environments are more difficult to practice kindness in, but it is always possible. When people are mean or resistant to your positive intentions, we must be able to recognize that it is not personal. Being a contrasting figure to a person's negative emotional patterns can create a conflict in their reality. By remaining objective and compassionate, we can keep our peace and not fuel their reaction. Another person's attitude is not your personal issue. By transforming your outlook you can diffuse your reaction and dissolve the acceleration of a conflict. This does not mean allowing someone to treat you poorly. This merely suggests that you acknowledge the other person's chosen discomfort within a disagreement, practice compassion for it, and respect that they are dealing with their issue in their own way. Respecting that everyone is having their own personal journey with their own perceptions grants you the freedom to honor your own journey in the same way. Don't allow an unhealthy perspective to corrupt your peace.

Sometimes people can be so nasty. I love them anyway. From time to time, someone's negative perspective will be inflicted on my reality and it makes my heart ache. I love them anyway. The truth is, *our* truth is, that these people, these situations, they look like they are separate from us, but I know this is not true. From the level of Being that I know well, these people, these things, despite the chaos and negativity, are us in various forms. The illusion of separateness causes this suffering. Although parts of my higher self walk around, sleepwalking, taking different forms, roles, and often provoke me to question my faith in humanity, I know the truth. There is only one of Us here.

I believe in humanity, and my faith in us is strong, undying. I believe in us, the collective conscious, a world of Divine playmates that hold the same godly flame that I do. No lesser, no greater. We are One. We are the cells in the body of God, and we are healing and we are waking up. We have this Divine power. Although my heart aches in compassion at alternate realities of suffering, I know all paths lead home and we are that home. We are the path, we are the traveler, we are the help, the light, the motivation, the direction, the home and destination.

When someone tries to poison my mind with a cruel reality, I see an opportunity for healing. I call upon my inner peace. I move in love. I am love, and thank God that love is the ultimate healer.

When you begin reacting and acting from the soul level, profound things happen. To give up faith in humanity is to give up on yourSelf. Lucky for you (us), that Self will never give up on you (us).

In the words and spirit of Mahatma Gandhi, if you look around and do not like what you see, "be the change you wish to see." Keep your focus positive. Have awareness of areas of the world and people who need healing, but see the bright side wherever you look. Let gratitude light the way. Be gentle with yourself and others. Ask yourself if you are loving with every motion, every breath. Claim your happiness. Be the example. You may not be able to change the world, but you can change yourself, and the world feels it. The world is watching. Many of us have begun to see what a real treasure life is. We can recognize the light of bliss and love. I pray that this awareness is the most contagious.

We came here to love, to know ourselves. We came here to play, experience, heal our collective soul. Don't forget your truth, *our* truth. If you ever feel lost, know that stillness speaks. There is nowhere to go except here, to awaken to the now, to awaken to what *is*.

There is something so beautiful and sacred in the connection of souls. It is as if everywhere that you stand together becomes holy ground. Whether it is a friendship, relationship, familial or otherwise, these connections should never be taken for granted. I always pour gratitude into the souls willing to hold space for others, especially during vulnerable times. I feel holding space for another to share their unfiltered, authentic self is precious. I am blessed to say I have a handful of people in my life that love this way.

The more authentic and loving we become, the more our relationships and our world reflect that. Dare to love and be loved, completely. This is how we heal humanity and the world.

A REUNION WITH AN OLD FRIEND, MASKED BY THE SHADOWS

"Whether you succeed or not is irrelevant, there is no such thing.
Making your unknown known is the important thing
--and keeping the unknown always beyond you."
-Georgia O'Keefe

Diary entry October 4, 2012

The heart is designed to withstand its breaking. The heart, however, never breaks in destruction, but instead, breaks in expansion. Over and over again, we break and shed the sorrow. Renowned conscious poet, Rumi once wrote, "The wound is where the light enters," and every time light shines on the dark shadows of our heart, it is changed forever. Shadows are the illusion of smallness, light expands and it is only in the acceptance of both shadow and light that we know the integration of all that is

This month marks my third year prescription drug free, and up until this past week, I was depression-free. Spirit, God, Goddess (whatever name you wish) has a Divinely timed way of presenting challenges, also known as opportunities for healing and awakening. My personal experience of the human condition has proven time and time again that I am never met with anything that I can't eventually overcome or transmute into something beneficial. This has less to do with the challenge presented and more to do with my state of Being as to how I choose to deal with the experience.

This time a certain series of triggers left me physically fatigued and emotionally drained. Not only was my relationship presenting challenges, the pressure of my job was increasing, the morality and integrity of the company was decreasing, I was also in the middle of moving into a new space with a new roommate after living several years on my own. Ultimately, a lot of change.

"Be like water" became my mantra, I tried to flow but soon I felt my riverbeds run dry in complete exhaustion. At this point, a Divinely timed familiar experience began to saturate me: Depression. But this time, it was different. It was similar in many ways, but at the core, I was different.

"Hello, I remember you." I said as I felt the heaviness pass through me. Unlike before, I was able to recognize that this feeling was passing through me. "I have depression passing through me," I'd say. This time I knew myself more intimately. I knew my heart more deeply. As I laid in bed every morning for a week, my alarm would sound at 9:30am and I'd snooze every eight minutes until 1:30pm. That was the time I had to muster up the strength to get ready for work. "I am healing," I'd say, still laying in bed.

You know depression's grip when you find it so painful to get out of bed that you even when you have to pee, you mentally try to figure out how to make that happen with the least effort. Is there a nearby trash can? Perhaps the bed is big enough that I can just pee on side and roll to the other. These ideas are embarrassing and disgusting to a mind devoid of depression, but to the mind in coils of mental anguish, these

100

options seem more inviting than actually moving.

I used to fight my depression, deny its existence while also mentally identifying with the doctor's diagnoses. "I am different this time," I thought, "I have changed." Spirit gave me the opportunity to look this shadow side of myself in the face and say, "Fear based realities are not mine anymore." I love my shadow as I love my light because they are but one in the same. I didn't used to love me, before, when the depression was deeply seeded, but I love me now, all of me, and I got a chance to experience something that allowed me to express my healing love to all parts of me.

Each day, I consciously checked in my heart center. Now, I keep it open and receptive. Before I knew the love of self, when I was feeling depressed, I'd shut down. Mentally, I'd deem myself a burden and undeserving of love. I would feel energetically responsible and didn't want to "contaminate" others with my toxic emotions. This is completely derived from ego and exactly the place the ego likes to isolate the soul. But every day, I stayed open, remembering my own loving nature and the generosity of the Universe. This is how the grace of God held me.   Although it was veiled by many illusions, my heart remained open and gracious to the gentleness of the Universe during this particularly challenging time. Leaving my heart opened allowed me to let the compassion of others help heal me. Historically I have had a difficult time receiving. I have always been more comfortable giving. I feel graciously humbled by experiencing my capacity for both, dissolving any pride that once guarded the doorway to my heart.

To my surprise, many Earth angels came to the rescue, reminding me of my own light. A friend of mine reminded me, "Rest and recharge, God needs his angels strong. Be still and let your wings heal, dear angel."

Although I had cried at work before, I had never exposed my emotions so vulnerably as I did last week. By honoring my emotions, I felt as though I was clearing emotions not only for myself but for all of those who felt they didn't have permission to cry or freedom to feel their feelings completely. Cracking open and exposing my sadness with my light, others arrived to the call of necessary heart healing and began to act in love. A coworker asked, "What do you do to cheer up the one who always is the one to brighten other's spirits?" It's not necessarily what you do, but how you do it, and how you heal anything is lovingly.

So many dear hearts have held space for me this week (I use the phrase "holding space" to refer to the ability for someone provide a safe space for someone to be vulnerable in with no fear of judgment or criticism). Most of them didn't need to say anything, but were helpful by just simply being present. I felt strongly the desire to be held, but in my fickle emotions, didn't really want to be touched. As I voiced this, I felt the loving embrace of the angels that I had felt a few times before. This was a place for me to fall apart, to heal, to mend my "broken" wings.

I don't have it all figured out today, but having vitality that I once did not was the super power that carries me through the journey of life. Vitality, self-love, compassion, and faith are tools for survival. Sometimes we have to break to be reborn. We don't break to shrink, we break to expand and grow even larger into our potential.

Surrender to the flow of all that is. By letting go, it all gets accomplished.

As I was writing this chapter, I considered not including it because it felt vulnerable. I know this is a necessary chapter because it honors the process of life. It honors and reveres the cycles that we experience in life, and with this diary entry, I share an authentic experience, as it was first written in the pages of a book meant for my eyes only.

I said in the beginning of this book that life does get better, and I truly believe that with all that I am. I feel that we are given opportunities to experience old conditions with new perspective to rise from the ashes of our wounded history. This suggests that the life does not necessarily start behaving differently in these situations, but it is with our power of perspective we can transform our life with great love and never look back again. Time does not heal all wounds, but perspective can.

INTEGRATION

"The sharing of joy, whether physical, emotional, psychic, or intellectual, forms a bridge between the sharers which can be the basis for understanding much of what is not shared between them, and lessens the threat of their difference."
-Audre Lorde

The human ego is a clever beast. At times I feel that our egos can help protect us by making small discernments and healthy decisions to steer clear of certain things. But like the comfort zone, there is not much growth in the land of ego-geared living, at least not the kind of growth I'd like to concern myself with.

Past observations of my own ego have opened my eyes to some room for growth. Like a garden, our human body and soul needs constant care and attention or things get a little unkempt, unbalanced. So as I have been pulling weeds, I have found how easy it is to the hide the parts of ourselves we deem unlovable. In fact, that is why the ego is so clever in nature: it is self serving. When we carry shame about qualities of ourselves, we send out vibrations that a part of us is unlovable. Therefore, it is hidden and treated less lovingly. As if this specific quality or attribute is the ugly duckling of our existence, we want to ignore, neglect, hide, or mock away this quality. The wise know this quality is yet a beautiful swan in the making. The qualities we are ashamed of need as much, if not more, light and love than any other aspect of our being, but we hide them, and without words tell the world that they can designate these qualities unlovable, too. This presents an experience of little growth, no transformation, and often times, stagnation.

We have all experienced insecurities. The funny part is that they are all in our head. If we reveal our insecurities up front and center stage, let a little light shine on them, healing can happen. Love happens. In fact, Love has already been happening, but by your willingness to bring attention to this unkempt garden, you are opening yourself to the healing nature of love to transform it. Sometimes this comes in a healthy perspective from a friend or stranger. Sometimes you realize, once you see this subject of insecurity in the light, it was not really anything to be afraid of at all.

So when you filter out parts of you because you want the loveable parts to be loved more, don't forget about the fruits that your entire garden bears. Let the light shine there too. You are *completely* lovable. You do not need time to transform your "ugly duckling", just a lens of perspective to see you have been a swan all along.

There is no battle between light and shadow, no war between sun and moon, no conflict of duality, unless you want to create one. Duality exists in Divine perfection helping us to learn and discover. Duality gives definition to what is expansive and infinite so we have a frame of perspective. Life is not about becoming more light and less dark, or more fearless in your shadow or more radiant in your light. It is not necessarily so polar, but this is how we learn the recipes for creation. Seeking grace and peace comes from balancing these aspects of ourselves and eventually transcending them completely.

When we are at peace within, we do not seek conflict outside of ourselves. Let duality dance beautifully within you to know your dimensions more deeply. Here you integrate infinitely and expansively, by dissolving the edges of form. When you focus more attention on this, or you show more resistance to these "parts", that is all there will appear to be. By allowing both to exist hand in hand you experience Divine union. Witness and subject cease to exist because they are one in the same, forever. Do you want to exist in parts, or do you want to dissolve into wholeness?

When you begin to see yourSelf (the God-Self in you) everywhere outside of you, everything begins to have life. Nothing is inanimate anymore, for you see your own Divine reflection in the simplest of perceived things. Staring at a tree is no longer staring at a tree but staring into the face of God. Life stops being ordinary and dull. You open to a world of magic. I am sure there are gradients of intensity in staring into the face of the Divine, but to some degree, I cannot help but to feel the intense presence of Self when I am Present with anything.

Trees don't speak like you and I do, but they do speak nonetheless. In fact, many of my writings are inspired by conversations with nature, including this chapter. Although I do not subscribe to all books of faith as one Divine truth, I do feel that there are some Divine truths that are interwoven into all of them that are often times lost in translation. In the Bible when God commands, "worship no gods before me," little do most readers understand that when you see God in everything you cannot help but worship the Divinity in all. There can be no other gods at the level of Being and conscious awareness; Only

sion of separateness do we fall into worship of the (addictions, habits, possessions, people as a form). .ed, every touch becomes a communion, every shared spa. a sacred temple. That is when you can see the Light in all things and treat them as if that is all you see. You can love something with all you are and also let it go, knowing that you can never lose something that you are, only something you have.

Many of the enlightened teachers and Ascended Masters acquired a total shift in consciousness that remained their active awareness, or level of consciousness, until their earthy demise when they transitioned into the afterlife. Many people invest in their spiritual work to acquire a similar state of Being. For many awakening souls, we are at a state of integration. To different degrees and variations we tap into a conscious state of Being and from time to time get caught up in a ego-based reaction until we, once again, dissolve the illusion.

Both points that hint at duality are also illusory. Words can only suggest or point to a conceptual state of God-consciousness because living in God-consciousness transcends the world of thought and the mind. It is omnipresent. It is everything and no-thing. It is everywhere and infinitely expanding. As infinitely as it expands outward, the journey inward goes even deeper. Although, in a God-conscious state of existence, there are no directions, boundaries, or prepositions. There just simple *is*, infinitely.

MANIFESTING HAPPINESS AND
A PATH TO PEACE

"There is no way to happiness --happiness is the way."
-Thich Nhat Hanh

From within, we create a magical exterior world. It is from our internal depths that we reflect the illusory exterior reality. If we don't like the dream we are living, we must wake up. Pinch yourself, you are dreaming! Pinch yourself with the inspiration to create something new.

How often do we doubt our dreams based on "failures" of the past? Failure can only happen if you claim it as that. By reframing the word failure, it can be used as a powerful motivator on your path to success and fulfillment. Often it is in these failures that we are redirected to the present moment for self referral. This is a place of deep communion with Spirit. The Present, also referred to as the Now, is the place where we can remember who we are and remember our purpose and passion.

Innately all of us came from a manifestation of love. Love is the needle, the thread, and the fabric of our creation . We can take this creativity of loving creation into our own being and use it to manifest our heart's desires. We are Divine, and once we recognize this within ourselves, we can begin to consciously co-create with the source of all Divinity. In the inspiring words of author Paulo Coelho, "When you want something, the whole Universe conspires to make it happen." Wake your dreams into reality.

Every person on this planet (and beyond) is a great magician. Every thought we make is magic. Some of us our conscious about the magic we're influencing, and others are mindlessly casting spells with thoughts. The trick is that our mind is incessantly full of thoughts, some assigned as "positive thoughts," and some considered "negative thoughts." I put quotations around this because at the level of Spirit, beyond duality, all happenings are neutral and every happening is transmuted into love. At the levels of form, the reality that we predominantly live in as humans, positivity and negativity does have an effect on our bodies. When we think positive thoughts, our bodies chemically change and the cells respond to our thoughts in patterns of health and healing. If we think negative thoughts, different energy is released and these cells act in an unhealthy way, signifying stress and disease in the body.

When setting the intention to attract what we want, we often fixate on the things we do not want and bring more of that our way. The first step toward correcting this, after awareness, is to practice positive thought replacement. To define *positive* in this context, I am referring to thoughts that create more ease, inspiration, creativity, love, and passion. Positive thoughts motivate us to pursue our goals and dreams, and fulfill us on the journey. Negative thoughts feel heavy and tend to weigh us down in our pursuit. Unlike positive and affirmative thoughts, negative thoughts tend to leave us feeling drained or unfulfilled.

When we recognize and replace our thoughts, we make a shift from unconscious creation to conscious service through thought. Unveiling the mask of damaging self-talk allows us to act from our witnessing consciousness. Witnessing awareness is a powerful ally in manifesting our desires. By separating our ego, we shed the mask deluding us from our true eternal Self. It is like living your life thinking you are a cloud only to realize that you are the entire sky.

Busy day? Bad traffic jam? Replace your thought with what your desired reality would be. For example, imagine the roads clearing, green lights illuminating the road, and that you have a parking spot with your name on it where you see yourself parking with ease. You're on your way to find it, and the Universe is conspiring to help. Rainy day when you were hoping for sun? Maybe it seems like rain, but it looks as though it is clearing up to me. It's almost like you can feel the sun on your face already. Focus on the desired outcome and it'll bring your affirmation to your reality. This is not a denial of reality, it is total acceptance of the present moment coexisting with self recognition of the power of your thoughts.

Now, I can imagine some of you are skeptical about projection. I had many of my own doubts long before I started living deliberately. "If this is so easy, why isn't everyone doing it?" Well, you see, we *are* doing it. We are creating our reality with every thought. Manifestations can happen consciously or unconsciously. Even those of us that are energetically conscious of our thoughts can have doubts when we don't immediately see results and then we bring a thought process of lack and doubt that hinders our desired affirmations.

Being aware of your thoughts is the most important step in manifesting your deepest desires. Oftentimes, you have to exercise what I call "super-awareness". When the doubts of others begin influencing your desired manifestations, you have to be extra aware to not adopt those dense, unproductive thoughts as your own. This is also why miracles take a little time.

Time and space are man-made concepts. In the spirit world, transcending duality, time is irrelevant and seemingly non-existent. Just imagine how dangerous it would be if every thought you had instantaneously came into fruition. Have you ever been extremely frustrated with someone and in the middle of the conflict wished harm to the opposing force? How awful and destructive it would be if that thought became form or action instantaneously? Spirit is on our side here and energetically hears every thought, that is why the garden of thought must be watered with intention. The more often we nourish our garden with intention, the more often blossoms brilliantly bloom. Our minds require maintenance, and an occasional weeding. When you are feeling frustrated with how long your dreams are taking to come to fruition, ask yourself what garden of thought are you watering: the flowers or the weeds? We could even go one step further and ask is a weed really a weed at all?

It is sometimes difficult to keep watering a patch of dirt faithfully when all you see is soil. You may doubt the seed's ability to blossom and that doubt stems from the doubt of your own capabilities. But how can you be incapable when you are both the dirt *and* the water, the sun and the seed, the growth and the dormancy? When you are tapped into the place that Spirit resides within you, this becomes more apparent, fear dissolves, and you see all things as possible.

In order to have a human experience, we voluntarily choose a temporary amnesia to walk about the physical world so that we can play, create, and experience. On our individual levels of consciousness, we may only see dirt or only see water, but our higher consciousness, the real Self, sees everything, because it *is* everything. Self sees both dormant seed and fully blossomed flower. It also sees the petals fall in full cycle. It sees all of this as you appear to be simply gazing at moist soil in the garden of thought. When you align yourself to the consciousness of Being, you begin to see these things manifest right before your eyes, too.

The saying, "Fake it until you make it," comes in handy here. If you were brought up to believe in only the things you can see, this may be more difficult to start and can feel extremely silly. It is with our child-like imagination that we remember our creative nature and birth our dreams. As Wayne Dyer once wrote, the truth is, "you will see it, when you believe it". I often encourage people to start with smaller manifestations to build confidence with this tool. Imagining things like an empty parking space in a busy lot when you are running late can quickly manifest the desired outcome if you dare to believe. This seed of confidence will blossom in your soul to inspire you to build bigger and braver creations.

Emotions, as well as music, have a particularly powerful resonance in the manifestation process. Thoughts become reality, but feelings become creation more rapidly. Feeling as if that reality already exists magnetizes the reality of that emotion. Feeling bliss magnetizes more bliss, and feeling depressed has its own spiral of manifestation.

Acting "as if" is one of the strongest signals in rippling our desires into reality. The only thing I have experienced to resonate with an even stronger potential is music and song. When I was a young girl, I would often sing my own theme music. I would make up verses as I went along, creating silly stories of mundane tasks I would be doing (I thank Disney movies for that). I could be singing about chores or food, and then sometimes I would sing about my dreams. Although I did have some voice training while I was getting my Bachelors in Theatre Arts, I am not much of a trained singer. Whether or not your voice is trained does not matter. This type of singing is its own best genre. I call this my Soul Song. I would sing my dreams into reality, not much differently than Disney Princesses sing that one day their Prince will come, only to be met with the subject of their song. Your song can be about anything.

Soul songs are not planned songs, they are improvised, although, if you are a song writer, ever better! For many years, the magic of this method was unknown to me; It was something I did without conscious intention in my youth. When I got into my early twenties, I had a roommate who, after months of observing my daily practices, said, "I know why you sing all the time." Not even realizing I did this with an audience, I replied, "Oh? Why is that?". She said, "Because the angels can hear you better when you are singing your prayers."

At the time I really didn't understand the depth of her comment, but the conversation sparked my interest to investigate further. Angels have always played a significant role in my life. As an adult I began meditating and meeting with my own guardian angels who helped me integrate many of my spiritual gifts into the world. Writing this book would be one of them. Upon investigation, I found that supposedly many others knew of the powerful vibrations songs delivered to aid in manifestation. Doreen Virtue, a gifted author and angel communicator, reflected on this spiritual tool and its significance in the angelic realms. She comments that, "Music serves to boost your manifestation powers. Music is part of the invisible realm, and is of a higher frequency than that of the physical plane. It wraps us in a protective shield to guard us from negative energies. It also lifts our emotions and thoughts to joyful levels."

The vibrations of song, dance, and instruments have enchanted us since the beginning of civilization. Before civilization, the Earth made her own music with water, wind, and nature. Churches, mosques, temples, tribal circles, all have songs or sounds that they sing to Spirit with intentions to worship, heal, or have their prayers heard. Songs are still a powerful medium of expression in society today. It is a gift that is available to almost any person who has a voice, and even those who can only hum or make sounds with instruments. We can set intention in that vibration.

Acting "as if" and singing your soul's song are powerful tools in making profound conscious intentions that you can radiate into your reality with the desire to manifest. Whether you are simply walking down the road, driving, doing chores, cooking, whether you have a seen or unseen audience, the vibrations of your song carry high frequency prayers into the realm of angels and into the rest of the seen world. It travels faster than dense worrisome and fear-based thoughts, and therefore the Law of Attraction responds in rapid manifestation. If you want love, sing or hum songs about the love you want. If you want abundance, healing, safety, sing the song that reflects that. Songs can invoke feelings in even the most emotionally detached members of our human family, and it is those feelings that encourage us to act consciously or unconsciously.

Pioneer of water research, Masaru Emoto unlocked a whole new awareness of the power of vibrations with his water molecule studies. Through his research he was able to show that water can retain memory or impressions from the surrounding environment. Through a series of experiments involving a variety of music, series of words, and different intentions, Emoto observed dramatic variations of structure of the water molecules based off of the influences of energy and sound. Rock music affected the water differently than classical music. The words, "Thank you" transformed the structure of the water molecule differently than the phrase, "You are an idiot." We and our world are primarily made of water and these molecules are in constant reaction to sounds, thoughts, intention, and attention. With this study, Emoto revealed through science what metaphysics has been claiming for centuries prior. This influence has been present since the beginning of thought and sound and has been shaping us and the world.

Our mind is our sanctuary. When we blame outside influences on our unhappiness, we must recognize it is only possible because we gave them permission to do so. Staying aligned with your Higher Self, or your truth, allows you to remain present when external situations have the potential to impact your mind with negative thoughts, and your emotions with negative reactions. Others do not make you "happy" or "unhappy". These are conditional versions of emotions. True happiness is an inside job and a choice we are given every moment. The only battle we are fighting is the one with ourselves. Others may uncover the blockages and areas for growth inside of us, but we must take the bait to be caught in the dynamic. There is a gate keeper of your mind that allows certain thoughts to enter and dissolves other thought forms at the gate. When you become alert to the trespasses of your mind and establish the source of emotion and thought, you are able to protect the sanctuary of your mind, and make mindful decisions with authentic reactions to contribute to the world around you.

Your ego may influence you otherwise, convincing you that a negative external circumstance is worthy of being upset over. Our egos justify suffering subconsciously and it is easy to adopt this perspective. What is really being translated by this external trigger are ideas such as, "I do not have enough," "this situation makes me less of who I am," "I want more and I am not getting my way," "this thing is threatening my identity," "I am right and they are wrong," "this is a personal offense." That is the core. Once the ego convinces the mind that the external trigger is a personal offense, you give the subject permission to transform your world.

When such negative sensations sneak into my conscious mind, I ask myself why I gave them permission to pass the guardian of my mind in the past. This allows an opportunity to clear something that I was once unaware of and now have the power to dissolve through awareness and conscious intention. Each of us has the power to choose happiness, and this is an ultimate super power.

If today was your last day in this lifetime, could you say you are doing something you want to do? Are you finding joy today, here and now? How many days has it been since you played? Are you spending your days feeling emotionally rich? Are you loving and appreciating?

I live my life in such a way that if someone exits stage left (metaphorically speaking) there is never a doubt that they were loved by me. Even in disagreements, or tense moments, I will always say, "I love you," (silently or aloud) and mean it with all that I am. I always go to bed with love in my heart and gratitude on my lips. Why? Because at the end of our lives, love is what matters. Joy, peace, expansion, and play are the essence of our Being. These are qualities and the essence of Spirit, therefore they are traits and experiences available to all of us. By living this way, there are no regrets and an infinite potential for healing.

So many days go by that we fill with obligation. Fill your days with inspiration! This is vitality. This is the fountain of youth. Your dreams are not necessarily the dreams of others, however, following your heart's desires will never leave you poor. Living your inspiration is the moment you align with total fulfillment. Inspiration is fulfillment in action. When we find courage to follow our bliss, our lives invite ease, abundance, and magical opportunities for expansion and solution.

Magic, for me, is not about cause and effect, or arriving at a destination. Magic is experiential. It is about living the process when you can only see your dreams in the heart of your third eye (The third eye is one of the seven chakra points located in the area of the pineal gland on our foreheads associated with intuition and prophetic foresight). Magic is in your intention, and when partnered with deliberate living, you can bring your dreams into reality. Choosing a thought or idea, and nourishing it like a loved one, is the playground of creation where you are intimately co-creating with the Source of all creation. In Conscious recognition that every thought is magic, and with every thought you are co-creating with God, Goddess, all there is, you perform miracles.

The difference between the magic and the mundane is realizing that everything you can think of is possible of manifesting. Mundane thoughts say, "I'll believe it when I see it." Magic knows, "I'll see it when I believe it." The magical ones own their power like a super power and give intentions to their thoughts. Nourish the garden of your mind with love, and you will have a loving reality of success, happiness, and peace. However, ignore your responsibility in co-creation, and allow others to walk through your mind and pollute your thoughts, and you will find a hostile reality.

Luckily, for me and for you, it is often the moment right before we lose hope that miracles occur. As our night vision is still adjusting and we reach around for a light switch, a brilliant and reliable sunrise kisses the horizon and our cheeks. It is always darkest before the dawn embraces us with its unconditional love and promises kept. Our faith in ourselves and the Universe is our tool in following our personal life path to unfold our dreams.

Pay attention: Everything that surrounds you is an instrument of the Universe and is guiding you in alignment with your ultimate calling.

Listen: Your inner voice nudges you in the direction of things that serve your highest good and guides you away from the things that no longer serve you.

Breathe: Be here now. Breathing deeply into the present moment is the closest to "real" there is. Sink into breath and Divine consciousness saturates your being.

Expect Miracles: They are already there waiting for your attention. Be careful not to attach yourself to the outcome because it can distract you from miracles of the present.

Believe and Wonder: When you believe and are open to wonder, you begin to see magic that surrounds you. It is as though faith is the corrective lens to true vision.

Pure intention is a more powerful creator than selfish motives. Love carries a powerful creative vibration and when love is the motivator of your endeavor, your desires manifest with much more ease and quickness. Selfish motives can also produce creation, but with lower frequency vibrations, seldom do these passions have a solid foundation or longevity. This is why, despite all of the chaos and disharmony we may see in society, there is a greater chance for love and peace to prevail.

WARNING: Birthing your dreams into reality will inspire others to do the same. It can also surface bitterness and jealousy in people who have not recognized their capacity to do the same. Don't let this keep you from following your heart.

When you shine as brightly as you do, there are going to be people out there trying to dull your light. These people are just unhappy with themselves and look for any person or situation to project this hate onto. One of the core agreements mentioned in Don Miguel Ruiz's *The Four Agreements* that I take to heart is that NOTHING is personal. Whether it is a compliment or a criticism, every word we speak is a projection of our life experience and how we judge ourselves according to that. These words speak of the speaker, not the subject, and not you.

Hurt people hurt people. That is why I feel it is so important to send love to the ones that hurt the most. People can be cruel; Love them anyway. Your life is not about receiving compliments or judgment, it is about your passion and what you love, your hopes and dreams, sharing in compassion, and making a beautiful difference. Not everyone is going to agree and that is fine. By not feeding into negative expressions or comments, these acts are powerless on your path. It's tough to play in this sandbox playground of the physical world with people who don't know how to be respectful. By not participating in shame talk or hate speak, you begin to immediately eliminate that negative element from your life and radiate a sense of peace globally. What an empowering position to be in. Do not let the ignorance of others dull your sparkle. You came here to be the best you can be, to know yourself more deeply, to experience, and to be happy.

What does happiness mean to you? How would you define it? It is helpful to explore your own personal definition of happiness to aspire to a life with more happy experiences.

Someone once asked me what it felt like to be truly happy. I had never really thought about it before and was not sure how to put it into words at first. After resting in the feeling of bliss for a moment, I said, "Happiness feels like having a key to hidden treasure, and only after years of searching, finding out there is no treasure to find, the treasure was searching for the key while holding it the whole time."

This is my happiness. What is yours?

Part 2:
AFFIRMING A BRIGHT FUTURE

An affirmation is a powerful tool in reshaping our reality and manifesting our desires. By focusing our attention and intention we direct our life with a new sense of self awareness and overcome any discouraging and self-deprecating thoughts conditioned by our past. The goal of affirmations is to focus more on what you want in your life to manifest more consciously co-created experiences. Start your day off reciting your daily affirmation and repeat as often as you feel inspired throughout the day. I have included thirty one days of affirmations and life transforming perspectives to help you get started on your path of affirming a bright and successful future. After experiencing a full month of positive affirmations, I encourage you to create your own unique affirmations that will continue to inspire you.

Day 1:
I am a magnet for loving, healthy relationships.

You are loveable, fully and completely, just as you are. You are a magnet to all things wonderful and deserve healthy relationships with friends, family, and partner(s). If you want to pour more manifesting intention into this mantra, take some time to write a list of what qualities you look for in your loving relationships with family, friends, and romantic partners. What does health feel like to you? Spend some time sitting comfortably with your eyes closed and visualize what health feels like in your body. Spend some time being your own best lover and write yourself a note of admiration just because you are worth it! Try not to focus too much on the aspects of your loved ones that frustrate you, although it is good to be aware of your likes and dislikes. Instead, write down all the qualities you celebrate in the people that are already in your life and trust that you will be attracting more people with those loving qualities.

Day 2:
I see every moment as a guru. All obstacles present an opportunity for growth.

Every moment we have a choice. We can choose to see the challenge in the opportunity or the opportunity in the challenge. Each experience we invite into our lives with Divine wisdom to deliver exactly the experience we want to grow. With each experience we become more wise and better equipped to thrive through future experiences. If you find yourself presented with an obstacle today, ask yourself to see the opportunity to learn. See yourself as the guru, or wise teacher, witnessing the guru of the experience. If you are having difficulty seeing the bright side, ask for help from your unseen helpers. May you open your eyes to see the opportunity to know yourself more deeply in the mystery we call life.

Day 3:
I trust myself and listen to my intuition.

Each of us has an intimate knowing that helps us navigate through life. Have you ever had a strange feeling in your stomach when you are doing something that you don't feel is right? Have you ever experienced chills or goose bumps when you feel you are on the right path? Your body has a unique way of communicating with you. When you begin to listen to that inner voice and witness the sensations you feel in your body you are using your intuition. You know yourself better than anybody else, don't relinquish your power to others by second guessing yourself with every opportunity to make a decision. Today, trust yourself in making a decision all on your own and witness how it feels in your body. This is your Higher Self's way of guiding you on your life path. The more you exercise this God-given gift, the more you experience grace and ease with every decision. You are smarter than you think you are! Give yourself a chance to prove it to yourself. It is ok to ask for help in life, but replace self doubt with inner knowing. Today, we trust ourselves by practicing self-referral.

Day 4:
I forgive myself in order to free myself from my past. I am grateful for the present moment and look forward to the future.

Forgiveness is one of the best gifts we can give ourselves in life. There is a grace associated with self-forgiveness that does not burden us with the pressure to change the past, but allows us to accept it and move forward. By practicing self-forgiveness we find it easier to forgive others. Forgiveness liberates our Being to fully experience the present moment without seeing it through the lens of past wounds. By surrendering the need to change our past regrets, we can look optimistically into the future and pursue our dreams free of guilt. Today we cut ties that bind us to the past and know we did the best we could at that time. Now that we have clearer insight, we move forward with a lighter heart.

Day 5:
I speak kindly to myself in moments of doubt and sadness. I remind myself of the truth of my accomplishments and my unlimited potential.

We experience life in the waves of duality. Sometimes it feels like we are on top of the world, and sometimes we experience challenges that leave us space to reevaluate life and what we truly want. In areas where we are experience doubt or maybe even fear, we must be gentle to ourselves and speak kindly as we would to a dear loved one in need. Today, take the time to write a list of your accomplishments, knowing that your next achievement is in the making. At the level of your soul you are whole and complete. While riding the waves to your infinite potential, make sure to enjoy the waves, celebrate yourself, and thank God and all your unseen helpers for guiding you along the way.

Day 6:
I am a masterpiece in progress. I accept myself completely: all roles, all emotions, all stages.

There is no better time than the present moment to love yourself completely. "I accept and love myself completely in its current state in order to heal and strengthen it for the future." Today we focus on the wholeness that we are and all the variety of ways that it is presented to us. We honor our emotions and give ourselves the freedom and right to explore the depths of our feelings without judgment. Regardless of financial status, level of health, validations of success or struggle, we see all aspects of our lives as important ingredients in this special and unique entrée that is our life. See yourself as both teacher and student, giver and recipient. Accept yourself and your journey and by doing so you give others inspiration to do the same. Everything is unfolding in perfect order like a delicate flower blossom opening to bloom. I love myself, raw and unfiltered, knowing my authentic self is the home and expression of my Being.

Day 7:
I am patient with myself and I allow myself the right of healing in Divine timing.

We exist in various stages and levels of health. Our mind, body, emotions, and spirit all have a unique level of health as they work in relationship with one another. In aspiration of alignment and balance of all of these things, we practice patience with ourselves. Instead of speaking of illness, focus on your healing by thanking the Divine energy of the Universe for helping you to be healthy and well. In times of perfect health, we are also healing. Healing does not require anything to be wrong or dis-eased. Healing is an evolution of ourselves from one state of being into a expansive sense of awareness of Self. We heal individually, and as a result heal humanity as a collective. Today we eliminate any pressure on ourselves to rush recovery and healing, and instead, practice gratitude and patience for the healing process. If you know healthy steps to take to assist in this process, participate in those activities. If you are unsure, ask for help from both a professional and your unseen helpers.

Day 8:
I am gentle with myself and take special consideration in comforting myself during challenging times.

Harsh language spoken in our thoughts may appear harmless, not spoken aloud. However, they have great power to poison us. Our thoughts become our reality, and during challenging or opportunistic times, we need to be especially mindful to be gentle with our thoughts. Take some time in meditation and throughout the day to check in with your thoughts as often as possible. Be sure to shower yourself with kindness and compassion to comfort yourself into a healthier mental state. If you have difficulty on your own, ask your Higher Self or angels to help you find healthy language that will heal, inspire, and empower you. You are doing the best you can at the present state of consciousness and as you expand in awareness, you will effortlessly find the solutions you seek.

Day 9:
I embrace change with ease.

Change is inevitable and we greet it everyday. Today we invite change with open hearts. We are open to the momentum and expansion that change can bring, surrendering what is old to claim what is new. We are passionate about the growth that change brings and have learned to ride the waves of change with great skill. Today we make friends with that which is unchanging, change itself.

Day 10:
I free myself of expectations to create space for life to pleasantly surprise me.

Yesterday we awakened to the ease of change and acknowledged the role in our evolution that it can bring. Although we can expect change, it is important that we free ourselves from the expectation of outcomes so we can appreciate the present moment. By liberating ourselves from the condition of past knowing, we allow life to surprise us. By freeing ourselves from expectations of others, we gift them the freedom to be as they are without pressuring them to be as we expect them to be. Take a moment to look at something familiar with new eyes as if you were looking at it for the first time. Reveal a sense of newness by putting faith in what is unknown.

Day 11:
I dream of wonderful things knowing that I am not given the ability to dream without also being granted the ability to make it come true.

Today is the day we explore our imagination. All of us are complete with an inner child that has not stopped dreaming. Even if we have matured into professionals and adults, there is a dream inside. What does your heart desire? Make a list, no holds barred, of everything you want even if it *seems* impossible. Spend some time daydreaming about how life would feel if these dreams come true. Imagine a string between you and each idea and see yourself pulling the string closer and closer. Feeling creative? Make a vision board displaying people, places, and things that you would like to experience in life. Put it somewhere you can see it everyday. Know that each time you look at this vision board you are stepping closer to your goal. Forget the how's; Align yourself with the end result.

Day 12:
I see something beautiful in everyone because we all represent a beautiful expression of Divine beauty.

What does beauty mean to you? Where do you see beauty and what does beauty feel like? Beauty has a lot less to do with what the eye can see, and has more to do with how we feel. By tapping into our own sense of beauty within, we clarify our lens of the world and see more beauty outside of us. Today, spend some time to notice something unique and beautiful in a stranger and gift them a sincere compliment based on your observation. Have you been judgmental of someone you love? Spend some time today reflecting on the beautiful qualities in that person. This is sometimes challenging, but very eye-opening. Notice how you feel reflecting on the beauty that is in everyone and in the same admiration, find the qualities in yourself that are beautiful.

Day 13:
I love myself and value the healthy relationship with myself.

"I love myself" is a phrase that is difficult for some to say. Some would even consider belittling a spirit in the discovery of self-love and dismiss it as arrogance. Self-love and arrogance are not compatible. Self-love, true self-love is unconditional. Self-love is not only a birthright, but a reward you have won against your ego. It is ok to love you! Don't let others make you feel small! You are beautiful, unique, and irreplaceable! All in all, no words I can say will be as satisfying as the day you discover these things for yourself. When you are able to love yourself, you will create a healthy relationship with yourself which extends to your relationships with every person you meet.

Day 14:

I do not judge others. I observe others with compassion and make healthy discernments in order to enrich my life with fulfillment.

Judging others creates a separateness between the judge and the subject. To judge is an action of ego that classifies someone as right and another as wrong. By dissolving judgment in our minds we can make educated decisions instead of emotionally reactive responses. We can accept that the best choice for us in an individual circumstance may differ for what is best for somebody else's path, and bless them equally. With compassion, we honor the path of others without personalizing it to our own agenda. We also give ourselves the freedom to make discernments without seeking validation from others. Today we celebrate what we have learned up until this point in our lives but remain humble acknowledging there is still much to be learned.

Day 15:
I respect my journey and the journey of others.

Today we open our minds to alternative routes that arrive at the same Home, and understand the capacity for many different roads to take us to the same destination. Much like yesterday's affirmation, we liberate ourselves from the need to be validated on our path. We listen to our own inner guidance to direct us in our unique journey and humbly recognize that others have their own inner voice guiding them that will not be the same as our own. Today we reflect on the choices we make in our life as well as the choices we make that effect the collective human family and do the best we can to make conscious discernments to move our life in a healthy, fulfilling direction.

Day 16:
I have faith in Divine timing.

Often times, when we do not arrive at a destination at the time we expected or planned, we consider ourselves late. Our mind can busy us with excuses as to why the timeline unfolded the way that it did that can delay us further, or we can trust. Today we trust that we are exactly where we need to be. If we are running late, we surrender our worry to Spirit and say "Thank you, Spirit, for helping me to arrive safely in Divine timing". When we don't happen to get things exactly when we want them, it is often a blessing. When in traffic, practice being present with the moment you are given and offer the thought that you are being protected in this perception of delay. If you have been waiting for an answer or dream to come into manifestation, remind yourself of the grace of Divine timing. Free yourself from the pressure of expectation. In retrospect, we will have new clarity and insight as to the reasons things unfold as they do.

Day 17:
I dismiss the things that no longer serve to better my life.

Identifying people, things, habits, and environments that do not serve to better your life is a significant way to repair those dynamics and prevent them from hindering your progress any further. Some people are easier to distance yourself from than others, and some habits are easier to break. Take some time to have a heart-to-heart with yourself today and honestly acknowledge what things are better to be left behind at this point in your life path. Make a list of things you no longer want to waste energy on and release any resistance and sense of needing to manipulate a situation to keep these hindrances in your life. Consider and implement tools to help you create new conditions in your life. This affirmation can also be practiced with new situations that arise throughout the day. By recognizing conversations or dynamics that don't fulfill you, you can find yourself liberating yourself from the web of unhealthy relations.

Day 18:
Acting in selfless service is my very nature.

Serving and giving possess an energy of gratitude, abundance, and compassion. We serve realizing that we have something to give, whether it is a kind deed, a smile, physical assistance, an object, advice, or charity work. When we are thankful for the abundance we have in our own lives, we desire to share it with others to enrich them with their own experience of abundance. Selfless service is the nature of our Being. Already feeling fulfilled, we do not seek fulfillment in the action of service. Our actions are genuine and free of expectation. Find creative ways to share blessings in your life. Practice random acts of kindness. Have faith that every kind deed creates a ripple that transforms into a wave of transformation in society. The more we share, the more we have.

Day 19:
I feel at home in the present moment.

In the present moment, there are no conflicts. The past has no power here, the future is not anxiously anticipated. Today we practice *being* instead of doing. Look at the world with new eyes today as you gently breathe in the space of the present. Witness the stillness as your mind has surrendered to your spirit. Any time you feel anxious or lose attention to your breath, take three deep breaths and return to your home in the Now. Spend some time in your meditation practice (start a new one if you don't have one) and make this a top priority, especially if you feel too busy to do it. Saturate yourself with newness, comfort, and peace. This is always available to you.

Day 20:
My life is rich in so many ways.

Even if you can't see it, you are saturated in abundance and the miracle of life. Today we claim this abundance and recognize it as our dominant reality. Throughout the day, recognize all the various forms of abundance in your life. Perhaps it is monetary riches, but don't limit your abundance to that. Abundance comes in forms of love, health, kindness, the gifts of nature and other unlimited sources. If someone opens a door for you, or even if you open a door for someone else, bask in gratitude and realization for the blessing of abundance that opportunity brought. Abundance is everywhere and infinitely expanding. Claim the richness of your life and the law of attraction with deliver even more things to be grateful for.

Day 21:
I am motivated and inspired by change in cycles, acknowledging that I am interconnected to all things.

Life exists in cyclical patterns. Life is not linear and does not end with finality. As nature exists in seasons, sunrises and sunsets, phases of the moon, we experience life in cycles, too. Today we honor the flow of life's cycles as they rise and subside. We practice non-resistance as we honor the death of various aspects of our life in order to experience the new. For a caterpillar to transform into a butterfly it must experience the part of the cycle in the cocoon. Whether your challenge is holding on to emotions in cycles, people in relationships, or environments you have outgrown, welcome the new knowing that what is meant for you will return to you. Today we say "Yes!" to the kaleidoscope of life.

Day 22:
I take time for tender moments with creatures great and small.

Animals are remarkable expressions of Spirit, just as we are. Like us, animals are sentient beings, as are trees, plants, and Earth itself. When we take moments to exchange in kindness and compassion with all the creatures of the Universe, we have a newfound sense of appreciation for something outside of ourselves. When we look deeply into another sentient being, we see ourselves reflected back in great beauty. We can learn a lot from our pet companions and nature. Take time to be present with creatures great and small and shower them with appreciation for what they give to the planet. Reflect on their way of life, how they express love, care for their families and community, feel pain, just as we do. Awaken a new sense of gratitude for the animal soul.

Day 23:

I surrender my need to have my path understood by others and honor my unique life mission.

Although our paths cross and intertwine and all lead to the same destination, we take unique journeys to get there. Many lessons can be learned on a detour, and sometimes a detour saves us from a rough road or dangerous conditions. In perfect trust we can see that we all have an illuminated path before us that we call our life. When we try to explain our special path to another, we must understand that they have not lived our lives from a first person perspective so they may not understand how we got to where we are now, nor understand why we want to go where we desire to. With this same acknowledgement we must honor that the same goes to us in our reflection of another's life. Today we liberate the need to be understood to continue on our unique, co-created life path.

Day 24:
I am no longer playing "small". I stand in my power and know my worth.

How often do you feel like your voice does not matter or that you cannot explain something as well as another person? In these moments, we have forgotten that we have a unique voice and that it is worthy of being heard. When we shy away from stepping into our full potential we are playing small. You did not come here to be small. You came here to share your vision and your voice. You came here to stand in your power. By knowing our worth, we inspire other people to do the same. You are worthy of love, abundance, success, peace, and happiness. Radiate in the space where your spirit dwells and express your unique perspective knowing that it deserves to be heard.

Day 25:
I cherish my ability to be a good listener, knowing there is always an opportunity to learn something new.

The more often we recite things we already know, the fewer opportunities we give ourselves to learn something new by listening. Listening is also a compassionate practice that honors the speaker as worthy of being heard. When you feel yourself interjecting your comments into the middle of someone else's story, remember your breath and become present with receiving what the other person is sharing. By interrupting people, we are not in the present moment. We are either recalling the past or traveling into futuristic thoughts. Today we practice gifting another with an ear to listen and open our minds to learn something new.

Day 26:
I dismiss obligatory settings and align my self with inspired productivity.

By removing action motivated by obligation, you discover your dance through inspiration. Of course, there are bills to pay and things that seem unavoidable, but every time we exchange a task that is draining and seemingly obligatory with a task that is fulfilling and inspiring we see our lives aligning with prosperity. Really practice tuning in to that inner voice and ask it for guidance. What do you want? What fulfills you? Trade a dull meeting for a passion that aids in encouraging a life aligned with your goals. Notice how much more energy you have. With more clarity, you will find that obligations were not as mandatory as they seemed, but simply a distraction in the process that felt safer than diving into the unknown of your dream path. You have a unique gift to bring to the world. Don't delay in living a more fulfilled life experience.

Day 27:
I am more than enough to thrive.

Some days we can question if we have enough to survive, but today we are transforming our barely-getting-by thoughts into that of abundance. You are whole and complete. You are equipped with all the necessary tools to achieve your biggest dreams. Even if we cannot see how, we know we are destined to thrive. The how's are not up to us. The how's are up to God and the unseen help of the Universe. As you recite this affirmation, close your eyes and feel the expansiveness of your Being. Imagine the stars in your hair, and your feet deeply rooted into the Earth. You are more than enough to get by, you are more than enough to thrive!

Day 28:
I am my own best lover first, and I allow myself to experience pleasure in every step of my day.

We are our own best lover. How we treat ourselves is how we teach others to treat us. In the enthusiasm of manifestation, treat yourself today by being the best lover you can imagine, but to yourself. Remind yourself what brings you pleasure and comfort and saturate yourself in the sensual nature of your passions. Shed past conditioning of shameful views of your sexuality and embrace the truth of how you enjoy being loved and romanced. Give yourself a foot massage, buy yourself flowers, take a long bath with candles lit, play some pleasurable music. Imagine the perfect date and act it out as best you can whether you have a partner or not. We are fully capable of diving deeply into the romantic stirring of our hearts to awaken lovers with the same passionate stirs. Trust your call for love will be answered.

Day 29:
I choose my battles wisely, making peace the priority in all my engagements.

In all of our interactions we have a choice. We have a choice to unite or to be right. We have a choice to speak and share what we know, or listen and learn something new. Energy flows where we direct our attention. Not all disagreements require an overt opposition. Silence speaks volumes. In conversations, ask yourself if what you have to contribute is encouraging peace or separateness. Are there ways for you to express your views compassionately? A person who finds conflict with many things has their attention vastly divided, but a person with great vision and clarity is destined to make a more focused impact in how they view the world. Actively listen, and remember that peace is always a more productive solution than war.

Day 30:

I love my life and celebrate my unique contribution to the world. I eagerly share my special gifts and honor the unique talents of others.

There would be far less growth and experience in the world if there was only one person on the planet. It is a great delight that there are so many people who possess unique talents and skill to share our life experiences with. Liberate the need to compete with others today and really celebrate what your gifts are at your current skill level. Whatever skill level you are at, or whatever your gift may be, humanity can benefit greatly from you sharing your unique abilities. Embracing what is unique about you expands the consciousness of humanity by allowing others to experience newness outside of themselves. Your life is one of a kind! You are one of a kind! Share what you are passionate about and ignite the passion of life in others. The love of life is the essence of vitality.

Day 31:
I am love. Love is me.

You and love are not separate. It is only in the illusion of perspective that we exist distantly from our source: love. You are loved beyond measure and acting in love is your very nature. Dissolve the boundaries that tethered your suffering and witness the interconnectedness you have with all beings, all things. Love never dies and your soul, the energy of Divine love, will never die. Allow yourself to stand in love as often as you can today, and always. Eat in love, breathe in love, act in love, sleep in love, BE in love. Cherish the intimacy of this connection between you and humanity. Know that this realization alone can profoundly heal the world in which we live and radiate great peace throughout the Universe.

A NOTE FROM THE AUTHOR

It is my Divine pleasure to offer this book to you. I have been writing this book for over three years and it wasn't until I recently quit my stressful full-time job to honor my path as a writer and healer that this book came together as it has in the last month. This book is an intimate expression of my journey thus far, at age 26, and I humbly acknowledge that the path ahead of me has many lessons to learn. I selflessly hope that as I share my personal stories of growth and the lessons I have gained in life that they some how help to enrich yours.

I am fascinated by the interconnectedness of all things, including the human family, and I am so grateful that you took the time to open your heart to this book. We all have a story to share and I encourage you to know your story is just as important and is a valuable asset to expanding the consciousness of humanity. If you are inspired to write, please share your voice. You never know who you can help.

I am endlessly grateful for all the helpful hearts and hands that contributed to making this book a reality. As much as I wanted to write this book as an expression, I wasn't as inspired to make it a reality until I was approached with such need for it in my community. After discussions with friends, family, and clients, I often heard, "When are you going to write a book? Seriously, you have some things that need to be shared with the world."

After the fifteenth time of getting this nudge from Spirit, I surrendered to the call and put pen to paper, then typed it all out for you to read. Writing this book was one of the most blissful, challenging, inspiring, and rewarding experiences of my life thus far. Knowing that I am not a master of any lesson, I humbly wrote this book as an eternal student of Spirit, honoring the differentiation between truth that is eternal, and knowledge that is experiential and subject to change.

Life is such a precious gift and a brave choice. I pray that this book helps you to find opportunities to shift from unrewarding perspectives to a clear lens of perspective that allows you to see the magic that life brings. May your life be blessed, fulfilling, infinitely abundant, and overflowing with love. I love you.

Namasté
The Divine in me recognizes the Divine in you

ABOUT THE AUTHOR

Samantha DeBruhl is a life enthusiast and new generation thinker. With a great sense of compassion, she aspires to remind others of their spiritual nature and infinite potential. She is a gifted intuitive and cares deeply about helping others embrace the miracle that life is. Samantha has a deep reverence for expressing her voice acknowledging that in many parts of the world women are not allowed to speak their truth. She uses her voice to empower others to know their voice and to share their hearts with intention of healing humanity and creating a more loving, peaceful, and fulfilling life experience. She presently lives in Santa Cruz, CA with her boyfriend and her therapy dog.

71417180R00095

Made in the USA
San Bernardino, CA
16 March 2018